CW01648779

Seen Too

Heart-Centred Women Share Their Story of How They Stepped Into Their Passion, Purpose & Power

A Collaboration Hosted by
Katherine Massey

SEEN TOO

Heart-Centred Women Share Their Story of How They Stepped Into Their Passion, Purpose & Power

Copyright © 2022 Katherine Massey
ISBN (paperback): 978-1-7398027-9-0

All Rights Reserved

All rights reserved. No portion of this book may be reproduced, stored in a retrieval system or transmitted at any time or by any means mechanical, electronic, photocopying, recording or otherwise without the prior written permission of the publisher.

The authors of the respective chapters within are reproduced here with permission, and with their individual rights asserted in accordance with the Copyright, Design and Patents Act 1988.

Published in the United Kingdom

Hosted by: Katherine Massey

Cover & interior design by: Michelle Catanach

Published with the support of TAUK Publishing

To my darling daughter Olivia.

The strongest, most inspiring woman in my life. Always my daughter, now my best friend.

Love Mum xx

Foreword

We're Advance Brighter Futures, a mental health charity with a big heart based in Wrexham. Our vision is to ensure that no individual experiencing mental health problems feels like they are on their own. As a small charity, we can reach people that larger, mainstream charities often can't. Focusing on highlighting people's strengths, our services include counselling, lifestyle coaching, training, and group activities. We're incredibly proud of our work in the community, but we couldn't do any of it without our supporters.

As a small local charity, any donation—no matter how big or small—means a lot to us. We're incredibly honoured to have been selected as the chosen charity for the book royalties of *Seen Too* and the money raised will go a long way to helping the people we support.

Zoe Whitehead

Business Development Officer

Connect With Advance Brighter Futures:

Email: info@abfwxm.co.uk
Telephone: 01978 364777
Website: www.advancebrighterfutureswrexham.co.uk

Charity number: 1089638

Contents

Introduction

My first collaboration book in 2021 was a huge success, giving fifteen women an opportunity to be seen and heard, inspiring other women around the world and letting them know that they are not alone.

Having successfully raised much-needed funds for a local charity I thought, can I do this again? And here we are with Seen Too, a collection of hope, courage and reflection. Each woman has experienced unique challenges in their past that ultimately framed their future, leading them to their passion and now life's purpose.

It's been very emotional, as I have been with the authors every step of the way as they have shared their vulnerability and fear of being seen. I am confident that these women now recognise the power of storytelling.

I invite you to get lost in the pages of this book and the journeys of these women who stepped forward to help you, too, to feel seen.

Love, Light and always Laughter

Katherine Massey

Visibility Queen

Miss X

By Wendy Stoneham

'I feel at ease with whatever will come, not because I am strong, but because this is part of life. It is nothing to be feared.' ~ Angelina Jolie

I woke in the night, in my son's bed, feeling hot. I had fallen asleep with him after reading a bedtime story. I had the feeling that my torso was damp, dripping wet even. I reached down through the neck of my nightie and swept it upwards over my body. I could feel the film of sweat transfer on to my hand. *God,* I thought, *that's a lot of sweat.* I raised my hand to my nose. It wasn't smelly, so that was a good thing. I hoped I wasn't coming down with anything.

I was thirty-eight when the night sweats started. At the time, I wasn't particularly worried, rather, a little puzzled as to why the sweats were happening more frequently. I did start to worry, however, when my mind started to play tricks on me. I would catch myself trying to put the iron in the fridge or discover that I'd put the home phone in my bag (instead of my mobile) and taken it to work. I felt a cloudiness in my head and often wondered if it was depression, having suffered from it in my twenties and with post-natal depression in my early thirties. But this felt different. It didn't feel dark; it felt like I was going slightly crazy.

I googled my symptoms and my research pointed to early menopause. I discussed this possibility with my doctor who dismissed it as I was 'too young' … but was I?

I had a weird and wonderful gynaecological past—my medical file was thick! In fact, one doctor told me my case would likely have been used for medical students' training. He must have seen the horror on my face and reassured me that I would have been known as 'Miss X', or something similar.

My gynaecological problems started as a child. I had woken up with a tummy ache. I had a dull pain low down on the right-hand side of my stomach. My mum thought I was trying to get the day off school because it was my ninth birthday. She got me dressed and waved me on my way. We lived in a ground floor flat in North London on the Fisherton Estate, built after World War One. The property had original sash windows and the seven blocks were built to form two squares with trees and benches for the residents to enjoy. I walked to school every morning with the children who lived in the flat above us. Their family were from Trinidad. They lived as an extended family—Stella, her cousins Nicola and Pauline, their father and grandma (everyone called her Grandma, including me). Grandma was such a character and was definitely in charge of her very full household. It was a very short walk to our school and, as Stella was older than her cousins and me, she kept us in line, ensuring that we got to school on time.

The pain in my tummy started to get stronger throughout the morning and I remember sitting outside the school office waiting for my mum to pick me up. I was taken to St. Mary's Hospital in Paddington as the pain had become more severe. The hospital ran lots of tests on me—we were there most of the day. I had my blood taken for the very first time that day. I screamed so loud that it echoed around the high ceilings of the room—my mum was so embarrassed.

The doctors were baffled as to what was causing me so much pain and decided that it could possibly be something wrong with my kidneys. My mum was crying as my paternal uncle had died of kidney failure on his seventeenth birthday—this news was a big worry to her. The hospital discharged me late in the evening and said they would be in touch with my results.

It wasn't my kidneys. The doctors didn't know what had caused my pain, which had subsided by the next day. I now suspect that it could have been something to do with my right ovary. I had started puberty young. I had small breasts and pubic hair by the age of ten. It wasn't a big deal to me then—a few girls in my class were at the same stage in their development—but I did start feeling ashamed about my new body when we moved to Swanley, Kent, just in time for the beginning of my last year in primary school.

I was one of the older children in my year due to my birthday being in September. I turned eleven a couple of weeks into the autumn term of '83. The girls in my class didn't seem to be at the same stage as me physically and I remember shaving off my small patch of pubic hair every time we had a swimming lesson. We all had to get ready in a communal changing room and I wasn't going to risk looking different to all the other girls. I was already struggling with our move to a new area, away from everything I'd known, all my friends and the school I'd loved.

My periods started the following August, a few weeks before I turned twelve and was just about to start secondary school. I always suffered terribly with cramps, even taking pain relief and using a hot water bottle. I'd be doubled-up in a ball for hours, waiting for the pain to become bearable.

I developed even more problems at around the age of sixteen. I was now in a relationship with a boy a couple of years older than me and working as an apprentice in a hairdresser's in Bromley. One day, I was washing one of our regular lady's hair. The sinks were placed so that you could shampoo from behind. I wasn't feeling too great and began to get hotter and hotter—I felt like I was going to pass out. I thought it was because I was wearing my bright red Sam suit with a black sleeveless turtleneck underneath. The salon was warm because of all the hairdryers on the go and the huge bright lights that lit up the shop.

Somehow, I managed to finish washing the client's hair and told the stylist that I needed to go to the toilet. This was situated at the back of the salon. It was a very small room and had metal bars at the tiny window. I remember the sun was streaming through the glass, giving the area a bit of an eerie feel.

By now, I was having stomach cramps and feeling very sick, with a feeling of diarrhoea being on the way. I can't tell you how long I was in the toilet, sitting hunched over my knees, but I could see I had started to bleed heavily. I felt bad that I was taking so long away from the salon when they were busy. I then felt something slip out of me and heard a small 'plop' as whatever it was hit the water. I peered between my legs and looked down into the toilet bowl, unsure what I was looking at. Deep down, I knew it had been the early stages of a growing 'baby'. I am now aware that I was likely around seven weeks pregnant and had had a miscarriage. I flushed the toilet, cleaned myself up and went back to work. I didn't tell anyone about what had happened (well, not for a while) or go to the doctors.

My periods were awful after this episode. I would bleed heavily and have to wear tampons and towels at the same time. My menstrual cycle was irregular and so painful. I remember sitting on my boyfriend's lap one afternoon in his mother's sitting room, laughing and joking, wearing a pair of cream cord ski pants. Suddenly, we were both covered in blood. I had no idea this bleed was on its way, and it was mortifying.

This teen romance finished after three years and eventually I entered into another long-term relationship, three months before my twentieth birthday. I didn't have a good lifestyle. I drank too much, dabbled in substances I shouldn't be taking and didn't eat enough—it was the early nineties, and I was working and partying hard.

My close friend had her first child, and I was starting to want a child myself—being chief babysitter had made me feel broody. But I was still plagued with gynae problems. Things had gone from bad to worse and I had to have several investigations which involved surgery. When the surgeons had opened me up, they saw that the lining of my womb was growing on the outside and attaching itself to my bowels—I had endometriosis. The surgeon cut away what he could, but I would have to come back for further surgery and laser treatment. This was in May. I was eventually scheduled for the second part of my treatment in December of the same year … but it wasn't as simple as they thought it would be.

Within those few months, things had been happening inside of me. Throughout the summer, I had been feeling 'off'. I couldn't drink alcohol like I had been able to (I could quite easily drink anyone under the table, before ending up there myself) and would be sick after just a couple of scotch and colas, my favourite tipple. I would also be sick the next day. It was like having morning sickness; however, all of the pregnancy tests I took were negative.

During the second round of surgery in December, the surgeons found that a large cyst had grown on my right ovary. It was the size of a baby's head. The cyst comprised bits of bone, hair, teeth and even talcum powder. The cyst was removed, causing me to lose my right ovary. I also had an infection in my womb which had to be treated with strong antibiotics. This infection left me with scarring on my left fallopian tube. So, here I was with a working left ovary but with a damaged tube, and the right fallopian tube in perfect condition but no ovary.

By the end of June '95, my relationship had run its course. In August of the same year, I got together with my future husband. We had known each other for around three months or so and, to be honest, we couldn't stand each other. But one Saturday night, a group of us from the local pub went clubbing. It was on this night that we ended up kissing in the club and going home together (and have been together ever since).

Over the following nine years, I had a number of miscarriages, some I probably wouldn't have been aware of if I hadn't tested so early after a missed period. I had one prolonged miscarriage which was extremely draining—an ectopic pregnancy which resulted in me losing my 'good' fallopian tube. I still had my left ovary, although I'd had surgery to remove a cyst from it so there was a possibility that it would have scarring on it, and I still had my damaged right tube.

Finally, we were given the chance to have a round of IVF treatment on the NHS which started in the summer of 2003. I had prepared for this by cutting back on my party lifestyle and reducing my drinking and any other unhealthy habits I had, including smoking. My husband (we married in 2000) had tried to do the same, although struggled more than me at this time.

Even the IVF treatment didn't go to plan. However, on the fifth of August 2003, I had two top quality eggs transferred into my womb. I gave birth to our much wanted and loved son in April 2004. Unfortunately, I had yet another ectopic pregnancy just over a year later which robbed me of my remaining fallopian tube. But at least we had been blessed with a child. We were not going to have any more treatment to expand our family—that life chapter was now well and truly closed.

My gynaecological history was the reason I thought that an early menopause was possible for me. Soon, the night sweats turned into day sweats. My hairline would be soaking wet and there would be drips running down my spine. My anxiety heightened, the skin on my arms would feel like ants were running up them, I couldn't sleep and, when I did, I had terrible nightmares and very vivid dreams. I would wake burning hot and shaking all over. I was an emotional wreck. Anything could make me cry—frustration, fear, anger. I was starting to feel as if I was in a bad mood—something or someone was always getting on my nerves. There were days when I felt fed up, cross and sad. But I had no reason to feel like this.

I had always been a doer, a really hard worker. I was on my son's school PTA, I volunteered at my church, and I was running my own cleaning business. But I kept getting ill. I had shingles several times and terrible flu-like coughs and colds. My weight fluctuated. What with all this going on and my low mood and anxiety, I became unreliable at work and in my social life.

I had blood test after blood test, but the doctor insisted that I wasn't menopausal and again said that I was too young. He put me on a low antidepressant even though I knew that this wasn't depression. My mental and physical health continued to deteriorate, and it was damaging my marriage, my friendships and my business.

One morning, I was watching This Morning and Dr Chris Steel was doing a segment on the menopause. He said that if you are having symptoms then you are starting your menopause journey. Blood tests were not accurate enough as it would depend on the time the blood was taken in your cycle. He spoke about a urine test you could buy which would tell you if your FSH levels were right. I ordered the little strip tests from Amazon and could not wait to see the results. I was so happy when they arrived. I ran straight into the downstairs toilet to do a test. The result?

I WAS in perimenopause! The relief swept over me, and I felt triumphant—I love being right!

The doctor still wouldn't give me anything different to help. He simply upped my antidepressant dose. So, I began researching menopause myself. I paid for life coaching, read books, and listened to anyone who spoke about their symptoms. I took high dosages of vitamins and primrose oil. I began looking after myself with early nights and naps in the day if I could. I don't drink alcohol very often now; I barely go out socially nowadays.

I was still emotional, and this affected my work life (combined with working with some really difficult characters). I had started work in early years education in 2015. After a terrible experience in not one but two early years settings, I decided to start my own business. I wanted to look after children and give them a good start in their educational journey, but I was fed up with people and their games and work politics. So, in October 2020, I became a childminder and opened my own little setting. I won't say it's been easy, but it's been a blessing to me. It's given me a freedom I didn't have being employed by someone.

I'm in a much better place now. I finally started taking HRT two-and-a-half years ago and I feel the most balanced I've ever been. I'm comfortable in my own skin and I don't really care that much about what others are thinking about me. Not everything is perfect but whose life is? I'm happy being perfectly imperfect!

About the Author

Wendy Stoneham runs her own early years childcare business in Swanley, Kent. She likes to think of herself as the 'hippy childminder', passionate about children learning through play, in the most holistic and child-led way possible.

Wendy also has a passion for supporting women who may struggle with their mental health, having suffered with depression, anxiety, PND and early menopause. She has been on a journey of self-discovery and is now studying to become a self-care mentor.

Connect with Wendy:

Facebook: www.facebook.com/wendy.stoneham
www.facebook.com/wendyshouseswanley
Instagram: www.instagram.com/wendyshouseswanley20

I'm Sorry, This Is Going to Hurt

By Sandra Miskimmin

'The only time you should ever look back is to see how far you've come.' ~ Mick Kremling

I sat in pain, looking into the doctor's eyes, praying for some answers. He looked at me. 'I don't know what is wrong with you,' he said. The tears started to flow. All my blood tests had come back clear, and nothing was showing up. Through my sobbing, I pleaded with him to find the cause of my pain. I was struggling so much. I knew something was wrong with me and I was terrified ... especially as I had something else to tell him.

A couple of months prior, I had visited another doctor from the practice because I was experiencing excruciating pain in my pelvic area. I'm not someone to run to the doctors so, when I do go, it's for something serious. The doctor barely looked up from his messy desk and snidely asked how he could help me. I told him about the pain I was in, and the conversation went something like this:

'How's your cycle?'

'Fine.'

'How's the water works?'

'Fine.'

'Oh, you must be constipated then?'

'I can assure you I am not constipated.'

'We will check you out for a urinary infection as I bet it's that, get you antibiotics and you'll be fine.'

I was horrified.

Now, as it happened, I did have a urinary infection. As a child I suffered from them, but in my heart, I knew that this pain had nothing to do with that. I left in tears and phoned my mum immediately. She could hardly make out what I was saying but managed to calm me down. The practice nurse had seen how upset I was, so followed me out of the surgery to comfort me. She recommended that I took time off work to rest and hopefully the pain would go.

I did. However, six weeks later I was back in the surgery with the same pain; this time, it was worse than ever. Thankfully, the new doctor was much more understanding. He did blood tests, examined me, and booked a follow-up appointment. That is where this story begins.

The blood tests came back clear. The doctor asked me to describe the pain to him again. I told him the best way to describe it was that, when I was getting out of the car, I felt as though my legs were being ripped apart. I was an area sales manager for a company and was travelling over six-hundred miles a week, jumping in and out of my car like a yo-yo. There were times I would get out and grab the side of the car, trying to catch my breath due to the pain.

The doctor smiled at me and said, 'Oh, I think you have pulled your groin muscles, that's easy to fix, just rest.' Initially I thought, great. Then I told him my other news. 'I'm pregnant.' The smiled dropped from his face.

'Oh, you are going to have a very unpleasant pregnancy,' he said.

My heart sank. He explained that due to the hormonal changes in my body, my pelvis and back would probably suffer.

No way, I thought. My first pregnancy was a breeze. How could this be so bad? I would cope…

I didn't. I was in bed from September and my son wasn't born until the end of March. I lived in agony every single day. The pain that I suffered before pregnancy was nothing in comparison. I lay in bed feeling a failure but trying to do the best for my baby. The only advice I received was to take pain killers to cope with the pain. That didn't sit right with me. I didn't want my baby to be exposed to the toxic chemicals in painkillers before he was even born.

I did what I could; it wasn't much, but I tried. My only relief was to lie in a bath. I would spend hours in it. It didn't matter that it had gone cold, it was my only saving grace. I couldn't get out of the bath myself, so I had to wait for my husband to help me out. I never ever thought that, at twenty-eight years of age, I would need someone to help me get out of a bath. It was such a slow process and so many times I had to say, 'Stop, that's going to hurt!'

Our 9lb 2.5oz baby arrived and I prayed that the pain would go away. I wanted to feel normal again. I rushed back to work as I felt guilty about being off for so long before the birth. That ended up being a disaster.

The company was undergoing changes. They had made a girl redundant and gave me most of her work. There I was with two young children, travelling (at this stage) nearly eight-hundred miles a week, and doing more work when I got home.

One morning, I got up and told my husband I couldn't go to work. He smiled and said, 'Don't be silly sweetheart, of course you can.'

'If I get into that car, I don't know where I'm going to put it. I feel like driving into a wall,' I replied.

He wrapped his arms around me; I broke down and went to bed. I never went back to that job.

Throughout those eighteen months, I battled with pain and my health. I didn't feel like me and my nervous breakdown proved something wasn't right. Looking back now, I was probably suffering from post-natal depression but hiding it from everyone, trying to be 'Supermom'.

I was trying to lose baby weight—dieting, bootcamps, personal trainers and slimming groups. I was failing at every one of them. I would either hurt my back again or I'd be so hungry that my mindset was, life is too short to live like this. As a result, my health was failing too. No one ever knew the extent of my pain. I hid it from everyone except my very close family.

I played the vibrant Sandra who distracted people with her warm and friendly smile, fancy shoes, sparkly jewellery, bright scarves, and smart dress. But inside I was crumbling. What people didn't see was emotional eating, stress eating and drinking, and lots of bed rest after events.

We moved to the countryside and thoughts of extending our family arose. We had land around us and only two kids to enjoy it. It would be a shame if others didn't get to enjoy it too. We had always put having more children off due to the risk to my back and pelvis. What if the same thing happened again? By now, I was self-employed in the direct sales industry and terrified of not earning money. I needed to work.

Luckily, the company that I worked in conjunction with put on a promotion. Me being me, I worked out a plan to maximise that promotion so that if I got pregnant, money wouldn't be an issue or a cause of stress. I smashed that promotion (second in the company) and my husband and I decided to start trying for a baby.

Thankfully, I fell pregnant really easily. We crossed our fingers that everything would go smoothly.

However, in a matter of weeks, I started to get pains in the front of my pelvis. I remember standing in line at an event and someone rushing over to me because they saw the colour drain from my face and thought I was going to faint. I was only six weeks pregnant at this stage.

I couldn't believe it was happening again. The grinding of the bones in my back became a common sound and, yet again, the only advice was to take painkillers. The midwives had never seen someone with these issues before and didn't know what to do. I eventually got crutches and back supports to help me, but it wasn't enough.

This time, the pain was beyond excruciating. I would have lived in the bath if I could. How I got through those months I will never know. There were days that my husband had to lift my legs to move them, to help me out of bed and dress me. There were many tears—both of pain and of frustration.

I used the words 'I can't', 'I'm too sore', 'that's going to hurt' so many times. The emotions attached to telling my family that I couldn't do things were heart breaking. Feelings of failure kept bubbling away inside, but I kept on going.

My birth story with my youngest is a whole other chapter as it was so horrific. The midwife couldn't grasp the pain I was in and kept insisting on things that hurt me even more, the worst being making me walk after just giving birth to a 9lb 10oz baby. I kept saying I couldn't as my legs didn't feel right but I was made to get off the bed and walk. Thankfully, a different midwife came into the delivery suite and immediately rushed over to me and grabbed me. She knew I was on the verge of collapsing.

I was sat in a wheelchair and pushed to the shower room. My husband knew I was in a really bad way as I allowed the midwife to undress and shower me. Normally, as a very private person, I would have insisted on doing it myself, but I was broken. I will never forget seeing my mum's face when she saw me being wheeled back up to the main ward. I, as normal, put on a brave face and kept saying, 'I'm fine, I'm just tired.'

Trying to move was agony. I couldn't reach my baby and needed someone to lift him onto me. My legs would not work properly for days. I was using crutches to get out of bed to get to the bathroom. Many times, I thought I would never make it. Four days later, I returned home.

Yet again, I tried to lose weight; yet again, I failed. I would end up starving myself and/or hurting my body. I thought I knew what I needed to do but nothing worked. I went to osteopaths, physiotherapy, chiropractors, and had Bowen Therapy. I got relief sometimes, but nothing helped long term. This went on for years.

At one stage, I went to another bootcamp in the hope that this one would be the one that worked. I stood on the scales, the personal trainer measured me, and then he gave me the shocking news that I was classed as clinically obese. I had a body fat percentage of 45%! Me?! Clinically obese?! Never in my life did I dream that I would be classed as that. I felt like crying. I was so embarrassed. I was the fit one at school, doing athletics, playing netball and never had an issue with my weight. How did I let myself get to this stage?

Looking back, I know why it happened. I'm a worker and just keep on going. But when it came to eating, there were times that I was too busy to eat. I would grab sugary foods, chocolate and coffee (with seven sachets of sugar in it) to keep me going. There were days, if I was stressed or hormonal, that I would consume a full packet of biscuits.

When I was trying to be healthy, I would eat a Muller Lite yoghurt, but I would crumble a dark chocolate digestive into it for the sugar rush. I couldn't survive without sugar … I was addicted. I didn't know how to break the habit.

I was now at my worst place health wise.

My back pain was a nightmare. Fear of hurting it ruled my life. I missed out on so much with my children during these years. I couldn't go for walks in the countryside in case I put my footing wrong. If that happened, I would be in bed for a week. There were times that even doing things around the house was challenging. Thankfully, my husband and children were always there to help and never complained.

My back would awaken me at night as I turned in bed. My upper and lower body would move independently of each other, and I would waken myself and my hubby with a sharp intake of breath and groan as the pain ripped through my body. And yet, I carried on. People never knew the extent of the agony of my day-to-day living.

I remember standing at the checkout in Tesco, bracing myself to continue emptying the trolley, when a gentleman tapped me on my shoulder and asked if he could help as I looked in so much pain. I turned to him with tears in my eyes and let him. Needing that help was soul-destroying—I couldn't even empty a trolley.

So, there I was in January 2013, thirty-nine years old and feeling awful, desperate to lose weight and feel more human again, knowing that my fortieth was just a year away. I was so desperate that I bought slimming pills off the internet. Guess what? They failed too. How did things get so bad for me?

I was obese, in agony, and my asthma and allergies were playing up; I had hay fever, migraines, digestive issues, hormonal issues and, in September of that year, I experienced numbness on my face and shingles.

My body was crying out for help, but I didn't know what to do.

Then, a friend mentioned that she was trying something new to help her to lose weight and help with her rheumatoid arthritis. When she told me about it, I laughed. I thought, here's another quick fix that won't work. How could a homeopathic remedy help you to lose weight?

I was so sceptical about it that I challenged everything she did. There had to be other reasons why she was losing weight and feeling better. I told her I would try it out and prove it wouldn't work as there was no way that what she was doing was going to help me to lose weight and break my sugar addiction.

So, I started it. I thought, this will definitely not work. I will be starving, miserable and craving chocolate.

But something was different.

I wasn't craving sugary foods. I was satisfied with what I was eating. I had energy and felt better mentally. I woke in the mornings feeling better. I stood on the scales a week later and I got off them in shock. They had to be wrong. I got back on, and it was showing the same result.

I had lost five pounds!

That had never happened before. I only ever lost a pound a week and I would have been miserable for every second. My mind couldn't compute this. How could I lose five pounds in one week when normally it would have taken at least five weeks in the past? What was going on? I thought, that's a fluke, it'll never last, next week I'll gain it all back. But I had committed to doing this programme for twenty-eight days, therefore I continued.

The next week, I lost three pounds which motivated me to keep going. In twenty-eight days, I had lost thirteen pounds.

I was ecstatic. I was starting to feel more like me again, the me from my early twenties. My back wasn't as sore. I finally felt that I could get back in control of my eating habits. Could this be the solution? Could this actually work long term?

I continued on my weight loss journey feeling very empowered. However, I wanted to know why this programme had worked when everything had failed before. I started to research food, nutrition, homeopathy, supplementation and natural living options. I spoke to functional practitioners to get answers. My brain was on overdrive. People started to ask me what I was doing as I was looking so well. Women wanted what I was doing.

I was reluctant to work with other women at the beginning. What if this didn't work for them? What if my success was a fluke? What if I couldn't help them after they had put their faith in me? My overthinking brain was in a tailspin.

Then, something was said to me which changed my focus.

What if I could help another woman to change their life? What if, by not sharing what I knew, someone would continue to live a life where they hated their body and lived in pain and suffering every day because I didn't share what I knew?

I couldn't live with that thought. I knew my future involved helping women.

I had to help women feel amazing. To give them back hope. To show women there was an alternative solution for their health. So, I started this new journey. For a couple of years, I was happy with what I was doing. However, there was something missing. Something was niggling away in my brain.

All my knowledge was self-researched and learned. I knew a lot, but I needed something more. I wanted to qualify officially in food, nutrition and weight loss so I could help more women. I spent a lot of time and money educating myself. I focused on the naturopathic ways of living and a holistic approach to the body. My mind was blown again.

For the first time in my life, I understood why I was having issues with my health and my weight. I knew why I kept failing. No one had ever put the pieces of my health jigsaw together. They only ever looked at one thing at a time. It was so much more than simply eating less and exercising more. I felt more empowered than ever to help women understand their body and help themselves to live their best lives possible.

At the time, I didn't know what my business was going to be called, but I woke up one morning with the word SMASH in my head. It brought my name and what I wanted to do together—Sandra

Miskimmin's Alternative Solutions for Health. My new business was born.

The traditional route to losing weight and regaining my health failed me and it fails many others too. For so long, we have been fed lies about what 'healthy' is. I want to educate women in a fun way to not only lead a healthy fulfilled life but to enable their children and the generations that come afterwards too.

We don't have to grow old and feel miserable. I am now forty-eight years old, and I have gone from someone who could barely empty a dishwasher or shopping trolley to someone who can use the gym regularly, play netball twice a week, and enjoy every minute of my life. I have no signs of perimenopause and I often get mistaken for being my daughter's sister, rather than her mummy.

So, what began as 'yet another diet' actually changed my life forever.

Little did I know, back in October 2013, that I would be able to stop saying the words, 'I'm sorry, this is going to hurt'.

Nowadays, it is more a case of, 'Let's do it. Let's SMASH it.'

About the Author

Sandra Miskimmin is the founder of SMASH Worldwide and helps women put the pieces of their health jigsaw back together so they can feel fantastic again. She believes every woman deserves to feel fantastic as they go through their life, rather than just trudging along, surviving. Sandra's mission is to help women fall in love with cooking again so they can jump out of bed each morning with boundless energy, ready to smash the day ahead.

Sandra lives in the west of Northern Ireland with her husband and is mum to three amazing children. You will find her in the kitchen creating new healthy recipes for everyone to enjoy, playing netball, in the gym or spending time in nature. She lives a very simple life preferring a more natural, alternative way of living.

Connect with Sandra:

Website: www.smashworldwide.com
Facebook: www.facebook.com/SMASHWorldwide
Instagram: www.instagram.com/SMASH_worldwide
LinkedIn: www.linkedin.com/in/sandramiskimmin

What's the Worst That Can Happen?

By Emma Semper-Hopkins

'Owning our story and loving ourselves through that process is the bravest thing that we'll ever do.' ~ Brené Brown

In 2017, I requested a meeting with my director. I sat waiting, a mixture of dread that I was letting them down and elation that I had finally made a brave decision. I was about to hand in my letter of resignation to the company where I had worked for over ten years.

This wasn't an easy decision to make. I'd held a successful career in corporate retail and worked my way up to senior management. I was managing a large team and felt secure having a monthly wage in the bank every month ... but something had to give.

You see, at the end of 2017, I'd reached a point of burnout. I was overwhelmed, emotional, not sleeping and not feeling good about anything as I was doing too much. I was a new mum, having recently returned to work after maternity leave, while also running my part-time upholstery business (which I'd set up during maternity leave). We were also in the process of renovating a chapel for the business which was situated next to my home.

On top of this, I was trying to be a good wife, find time for me, and balance many spinning plates. Trying to do everything had me believe I wasn't good at doing anything and I needed to stop something … but what? So, I sat down with my boss and asked for help. I asked if there was any support and to speak to someone independent like a counsellor so there was no judgement. It wasn't like I couldn't speak to my family openly, but I didn't want their thoughts to affect my decision.

'Ask for help. Not because you are weak. But because you want to remain strong.' ~ Les Brown

After six sessions with the counsellor, the one question that sticks in my mind, even now, is: what's the worst that can happen?

What's the worst that can happen if you leave your career behind for a brand-new venture?

She asked the same question to many of the thoughts and fears that had consumed my mind for months, including the financial impact and the additional strain that it could put on my family.

What's the worst that can happen and what can you do about it?

When you put it in simple terms you can take a much more objective, rational view. Of course, it's easy to think that now, rather than in the moment when your brain is in a complete fog because there is too much going on. So, step back and take a deep breath!

***

Looking back, I realise that throughout my life I've done things to please other people without considering my own needs. I think a lot of us fall into this trap, and then in hindsight think, *why did I do that?*

'Self-care is never a selfish act—it is simply good stewardship of the only gift I have, the gift I was put on earth to offer to others.' ~ Parker Palmer

In some ways, I was doing everything *but* looking after myself. Now, I truly understand why the air stewardess always tells you to put your mask on first before you help anyone else—you are no use to anyone if you don't look after yourself first. This means *truly* putting your needs first and implementing changes, rather than simply making a decision and then taking no action. Otherwise, it becomes a vicious circle.

After those counselling sessions, I decided to hand in my notice. I did this with the full support of my family. I was excited to see where my new business would take me.

I Still Didn't Feel Like Me

The next three years whizzed by while setting up and growing the business. I appreciated the flexibility that it brought me to have time to enjoy my young family. I was extremely grateful that we had a brilliant life, a beautiful family, a great career and business I was proud of, a home that we had renovated and loved … yet I still didn't feel like me.

Normally a very hardworking, positive person with boundless energy, I was exhausted again. I was constantly tired, over emotional and anxious. I didn't have the words to articulate how I felt. I was bottling everything up and the slightest thing could trigger my anxiety. Not being able to share how I felt with my closest family was also very isolating. They knew something was wrong, yet I kept pushing them away. I wasn't able to explain how I genuinely felt without getting upset and was worried what they would think or take in the wrong way.

I had a constant urge to escape and the only way I could control these feelings was by walking. I would go out into the open air to clear my head. It was a way of coping, but it wasn't truly a fix. I was caught in a never-ending cycle. In May 2020, I hit an all-time emotional low. I needed some help.

I Discovered Hypnotherapy

In September 2019, I discovered hypnotherapy. I'd had a fear of appearing on video—live or pre-recorded—because I was worried what people might think of me and of making a fool of myself. Live video was a big part of social media marketing, and I was holding myself and the business back. I met Suzanne, a hypnotherapist and coach, in a social media mentoring group. She was offering a hypnotherapy session to get over the fear of appearing on video. I had never tried it before, but I thought, *what's the worst that can happen?*

I had a ninety-minute session with Suzanne via Zoom. We chatted a little to see what I wanted to get out of it. We also talked about me, my personality, and what was making me feel the way I did. Suzanne asked if I was highly sensitive. Initially, I didn't understand what she meant until she explained the characteristics of a highly sensitive person (HSP). The session included a hypnotherapy recording that I took away and listened to for the next two weeks. It worked. One day, I thought, *I'm going to do a live video today*. And I did. I didn't overthink it, I simply pressed record then posted to my social media account. Now, live videos are a key part of my weekly marketing activity.

Discovering I Was Highly Sensitive—What Does This Mean?

Suzanne and I chatted through some of the characteristics of a HSP and went through a questionnaire to determine if you identify as one. I did. Everything made complete sense. This wasn't simply a 'label'; it helped me to understand more about who I am and why I do things the way that I do. It gave me clarity. I now use my sensitivity to my strength rather than thinking there is something wrong with me.

Going Back To Hypnotherapy

After that initial session in 2019, a further nine months passed before I signed up for four more sessions with Suzanne. I just wanted to feel like me again and wake up happy and full of energy rather than tired and sluggish. I wanted to learn how to relax. I wanted to learn how to switch feelings off (even though I know you can't just get rid of your emotions and thoughts; it's about identifying the trigger and managing it before it reaches the tipping point).

One of the characteristics of a HSP is being a forward thinker. This is a great trait to have but it is also mentally exhausting. I wanted to find a way to work it to its best potential rather than draining me of all my energy. I wanted to be able to communicate better with the people around me, including my nearest and dearest. I needed to be honest rather than internalising everything. I wasn't sharing how I was feeling; I didn't want to overburden people, and worried about their reaction.

Another hurdle I had to get over was spending money on myself. I've never had a problem buying physical items, but when it came to spending money on something less tangible, it was a hard decision to make. I needed to realise that I was worth the investment and stop seeking permission from others.

I had three of the four sessions during the summer of 2020. I saw a difference within weeks! How? I made time to listen to the audio recordings and implemented small changes. I identified previous situations and reflected on what I could have done differently so as not to repeat the pattern, learning what could have been a trigger previously. None of this is a quick fix—life is a journey and new chapters open every single day. For me, it's been a journey of self-discovery and taking the time to learn more about how I tick and how to take care of me.

There are many options out there to get help, e.g., coaches, counsellors, healers, journaling etc. Don't just follow what someone else has done. Hypnotherapy worked for me but there may be a different pathway to healing for you. Do your research so that you can make your own decision. Recognising what you are looking for is the first step to take.

Regaining Clarity and My Vision

In January 2021, I did my first ever vision board exercise. One good thing that came out of lockdown was that it gave us back time! By slowing down and having more time together as a family, we thrived. I had time to focus and identify what did and didn't make me happy, making plans to do more of the things that did and eliminating the things that didn't. It was a great exercise to do as a couple as I could physically show Dave all the ideas and plans that would usually be swimming around in my head. We set goals and dreams that we could strive to achieve together, as well as things that I wanted to do myself.

'No one else holds the vision for my life but me.' ~ America Ferrera

Previously, Dave and I would only ever talk about ideas, yet they would never amount to anything beyond a conversation—as a high achiever wanting to see results, I found this frustrating. By having shared goals, I stopped getting frustrated. I could see we were making progress—we made some big decisions that would have previously remained as dreams. One of these was investing in a motorhome, which gave us the freedom to travel (which had been taken away through lockdown). We've had so many adventures in Wally the Wagon, building beautiful memories.

'It is so important to take time for yourself and find clarity. The most important relationship is the one you have with yourself.'
~ Diane Von Furstenberg

I wouldn't be without vision boarding in my selfcare toolbox now. I've since updated the first vision board, proudly looking back at how much we have achieved. I've also carried out the same exercise on my business. I've never felt so focused and clear on where I want to be. I don't have all the answers, I still have days and moments when self-doubt creeps in, but I go back to my dreams and goals and those thoughts disappear because now, I have faith.

'Faith is a place of mystery, where we find the courage to believe in what we cannot see and the strength to let go of our fear of uncertainty.'
~ Brené Brown

Your relationship with yourself will never end; it's a lifelong relationship that will need to be nurtured. Life isn't perfect, and you aren't always ready for everything. Recognising that you want to change is the first step to breaking habits and making small changes. Now, I can see the positive results. I can finally say that I truly feel like me!

One of my biggest achievements is finally giving myself the recognition that I'm doing a great job—this is where true growth comes from. Gone are the voices in my head telling me that I'm not good at anything! I'm learning to take my nearest and dearest on the journey with me—I'm not doing it alone.

I now love the feeling of being brave and saying yes to opportunities. This is the year that I'm pushing my boundaries and taking myself out of my comfort zone—I've finally learnt what to do if I push myself too far.

I hope my story inspires one reader out there to be brave, courageous and to be you… .

What's the worst that can happen?

About the Author

Emma Semper-Hopkins is the owner and director of Semper Hopkins Upholstery and Interiors, a furniture design and custom upholstery business. She specialises in chair transformations, teaching upholstery workshops and custom made industrial furniture design. Seeing the sense of fulfilment and joy that clients achieve from making a piece of furniture from a set of materials is what she appreciates the most, as well as transforming period chairs for her clients.

Emma lives in Scholar Green, Cheshire, with her husband Dave and son Alfie. She enjoys travelling with her family, appreciating the freedom, fun and experience that it brings. In her spare time, she enjoys walking or doing creative crafty experiences.

Connect with Emma:

Email: hello@shupholstery.co.uk
Facebook: www.facebook.com/shupholstery
Instagram: www.instagram.com/sh_upholstery

Becoming Me

By Samina Rai

'Courage isn't having the strength to go on – it is going on when you don't have strength.' ~ Napoléon Bonaparte

It was a Friday morning like any other. The morning traffic was a familiar sight as I drove to school for another day of teaching. The congestion close to school was manic. I entered the busy roundabout with caution. Was there another incident? Almost immediately after this thought, my car was shunted in the rear.

No! This can't be happening! I'm in the middle of a roundabout, how can I step out of the car? I'm going to be late!

My heart pounded as all these thoughts raced through my mind. I suddenly switched into action, grabbed my phone and bravely stepped out of my car. As I observed the damage the other driver came charging towards me, yelling at me to get out of the way. I tried to speak to him about exchanging details, but he was not interested. The traffic had locked us into a tight spot—he couldn't get away unless I moved. He was trapped.

His behaviour prompted me to take a photo of our cars. He stood in front of his car to block his number plate and prevent me from capturing it in the shot. I took the picture anyway. Completely shaken by his behaviour, I memorised his number plate. He then angrily tore his number plate off the front of his car and threw it onto the back seat. I noticed a young woman was sat in the passenger seat, witnessing all of this. I knew talking to the driver wasn't going to work and, by this point, I was trembling from his verbal abuse. I frantically hopped back into my car and drove to work, shaking, while repeatedly saying his number plate out loud so as not to forget it.

As I arrived at school, I noted the number plate on my phone and, shaken up, made my way into class. As soon as I met my colleague, I burst into tears and shared what had happened. She was horrified. I quickly wiped the tears away as the children were about to come in. I braced myself with a smile to deliver an assembly to the juniors. No one suspected anything. I was so used to burying my emotions that I didn't think twice about it until my deputy head met me later (after hearing what had happened) and told me I shouldn't even be in work. The truth sank in—I had experienced a hit and run.

I don't know how I got through that day—it was all a blur. It's only when I arrived home and sat down on the couch that I started to feel the impact of what had happened. I felt exhausted and fearful. *What do I do next?* I asked myself. The other driver and I didn't exchange details. Perhaps he didn't have any insurance.

A part of me felt a strong sense of injustice—a value I carried strongly. The anger within got stronger. I knew I had to report the incident to the police. They did not follow up with the driver involved, though they did provide his details. My insurer dealt with the case. The key piece of evidence which supported my claim was the photo of his car up against mine.

Life appeared to return to normal except for one thing: I began to have nightmares and noticed myself on edge when I was driving. Two years later, it transpired that I had some symptoms of post-traumatic stress disorder (PTSD). I was referred to a therapist to help me overcome the effects of the incident.

No More Hiding

One day, I turned up as usual for my session and my therapist gave me a prolonged look. This time, something was different. She said something along the lines of, 'I think there are other factors affecting you.'

I paused for a moment and replied, 'Yes, there are.'

My therapist looked me in the eye as if she knew my secret. She knew there was more pain behind my symptoms. I wasn't able to hide from her. I couldn't deny the truth of what had happened to me … that I grew up without my mother due to her abandoning me at the age of eighteen months. It left me feeling unwanted and unloved. I pushed these experiences aside as something that belonged to the past. Yet it seems they were very much alive in me. This conversation led to my decision to continue my healing journey. I never looked back, other than to reflect on how my past wounds were showing up in the present. It was as if the therapist and I were meant to connect.

On the outside, I had everything going for me. A great job working as an intervention teacher. A busy social life with lots of friends. Regular quality time with my family including my beautiful nieces and nephews. I helped run a charity supplementary school on my weekends. I oversaw a complete renovation of my home in just over six weeks. I was operating at a hundred miles an hour—whatever I put my mind to I would find a way to achieve it.

Behind the scenes, I struggled to get up in the mornings. I had to push myself with a great deal of effort to get to work. I often experienced brain fog and difficulty concentrating on simple tasks. Reading would leave me mentally fatigued. I also experienced difficulties connecting with others and often felt like an outsider. My struggle to get into work was being noticed by my boss—I was there by the skin of my teeth every day. When I explained my personal challenges there was little support or understanding. The thing is, once I was at work I worked hard and delivered my best. I got results for my pupils, and they thrived working with me. This was my saving grace.

Meeting Mum

I started a search to find my mum in my early twenties, initially scouring marriage records at a library. I asked family friends if they knew of her location. The last time I met Mum I was seven and the contact ended abruptly. Eventually, I heard about the Salvation Army tracing service so I sent off an application to them.

One night, I had an unusual dream. I dreamt about my mum, and she happened to be a hairdresser. The next morning, I collected the post and noticed a letter addressed to me. It was from the Salvation Army. My nerves escalated as I opened the envelope. My mum had been located. There was a letter from her with a phone number. I read it several times to take it in. I felt excited and nervous at the same time. This was it—I would finally get to meet her. I felt hope reading her words, expressing how much she looked forward to meeting me too. I didn't hesitate to call her, and we arranged to meet the same day.

I'll never forget that day. I walked into a busy café and my eyes were drawn to a woman in the distance. Simultaneously, she stood up as though it was me she was waiting for. I walked over to her, and she called out my name. We embraced each other and shed some tears. We sat down and shared random things about ourselves and discovered both of us disliked coffee. Then she mentioned she owned a hairdressing salon. I was surprised. I told her about my dream though she didn't respond. I thought nothing of it. There was a distance between us which I hoped would change over time.

We met a few times and each time felt equally distant—there was a lack of emotional connection. What bothered me the most was the fact that I felt like a secret in her life. I was instructed to only contact her Monday to Friday between 9am and 3.30pm. It made me wonder if she had mentioned meeting me to her family. She said she told her daughter and husband, just not her son. I didn't dare question it and, in hindsight, I think it was out of fear of losing her again. I desperately wanted things to work out.

It felt like such a fragile relationship when I was told I looked like my father, a hint of disappointment in my mum's voice. Her unresolved emotions from the past were preventing us from getting closer. One day, we had a misunderstanding during a phone call which ended abruptly and so did the communication.

Five years later, I reached out to my mum in the hope we could make it work this time. She agreed to meet for dinner. I was told not to take things the wrong way, but my sister didn't want to know me. I felt deeply disappointed. Mum gave me hope by sharing that she would love to invite me over to her house to stay. Then, she looked me in the eye and told me she had no feelings for me. I felt numb and confused. I dismissed everything which hurt me like it was no big deal, and we left the meal agreeing to meet again.

Three weeks later, I received a text from my mum telling me she was no longer interested in staying in touch. I couldn't believe what I was reading. I questioned why. All I received was a text back saying, 'This is my last text, have a happy life, goodbye.' I've never forgotten those words ever since.

Prior to meeting my mum, I held on to a childlike fantasy of having an instant connection with her. Someone I could see myself in. Someone who gets me. The best friend I was always looking for. I just wanted my mum to love me and for me to love her back.

Why Did All This Happen?

During the first three years of my healing journey, I went through extreme energy crashes every evening after work. It felt like a rollercoaster and took every ounce of strength to keep going. I didn't have the energy to cook on most days and heavily relied on school lunches for my only hot meal of the day.

I learnt that the body holds the story of our lives. Trauma can dysregulate our nervous system and this stress can take its toll and lead to sickness. I tried almost every modality suggested by a trauma expert on my healing journey. Some worked better than others. I started to learn how and why trauma gets stuck. I discovered the benefits of neuroplasticity and Polyvagal theory.

As I began to feel better and let go of many shackles from the past, I began to question why I went through so many challenges from such an early age in my life. I often spoke to God and asked why. The answer that kept coming back to me was that I was meant to help others. I had so much knowledge and experience that I felt it would be a disservice not to share it.

And so, in 2019, I began training in several modalities. I quit my sixteen-year teaching career to start my business helping other women to heal from trauma.

The Lessons And The Gifts

Following the hit and run, I experienced so many transformational changes and 'aha' moments. It was a journey I never anticipated taking; a journey filled with pain, grief, hope and joy. I recovered from depression. The nightmares and flashbacks subsided. My nervous system became regulated, and the irritable-bowel syndrome (IBS) disappeared. I could finally feel the brain fog lift. I could read and study more easily. My concentration continued to improve. People who no longer resonated with me drifted away and new people entered my life.

My ability to connect with others grew. Finally, I knew that the love I was seeking was inside me all along. I developed compassion towards myself. I could feel my emotions in a way I hadn't experienced before. I learnt that I wasn't broken. I was, in fact, a survivor and thriver. I was always loveable and worthy of love. Love was always available to me through God and through myself.

The biggest reason I am where I am today was my ultimate faith in God to help me heal. My faith helped me to persevere through my darkest moments. I often recalled this quote: 'Allah (God) did not send down a disease without having sent down its cure.' ~ Prophet Muhammed (peace be upon him).

I have a strong intuition and an ability to quickly understand the root cause of people's issues and what they need to support their healing. This was the gift my experiences delivered. I celebrate eight years into my healing journey as I write this. My journey and learning continue as I strive to deliver the best that I can to those I'm privileged to work with.

What I find incredibly inspiring is how radically people blossom. They become who they were meant to be. I get to witness these transformations all the time. We humans have so much resilience and adaptability to be able to endure so much suffering and still come out the other end, not only to survive but with the potential to thrive. This is what post-traumatic growth is all about—thriving!

Time Is Not A Healer

My message to others is to avoid suppressing your emotions. Ignoring the body's warning signs can lead to burnout or illness. You must feel the emotions you're experiencing so that you can let them go. Time is not a healer. Any past experiences which are unprocessed linger in the body and can get triggered anytime your brain thinks it is re-experiencing a similar threat. Notice any reoccurring patterns in your life. There's a reason why they are happening and present an opportunity for change. You can't change what you don't understand. Ask yourself where these patterns are coming from.

And so, the hit and run incident which shook me to my core turned out to be one of the biggest blessings of my life. It was the catalyst to my healing journey. My mum's abandonment of me is where my purpose truly began. My life experiences were moulding me into the woman I needed to become in order to guide other women to heal their attachment wounds and break the trauma cycle.

I'm not going to pretend this journey was easy, though what I can say is it was worth it. You can reinvent yourself at any time, let go of the fear and operate from a place of love. The beauty about healing is that you can let go of the pain and forgive those who hurt you. The compassion which fills your heart opens up a new level of emotional freedom—the freedom to be YOU knowing you have always been good enough and loveable.

About the Author

Samina Rai is a writer, healer and speaker. She is passionate about inspiring women to heal trauma at the root cause so they can embody self-love and create healthier relationships. She advocates the importance of healing attachment wounds to experience true joy in relationships and life as a result of having the courage to address that which they may have suppressed.

She hopes to inspire others through her own journey of re-discovering her worth after early maternal abandonment. This journey led to her calling. She utilises the power of working with the body and mind as a foundation for deep healing. She offers various programs which move women along their journey from trauma to thriving in their health and relationships. In her spare time, she enjoys exploring different cultures through her passion for travel.

Connect with Samina:

Email: samina@saminarai.com

Website: www.saminarai.com

Instagram: www.instagram.com/saminarai_

Facebook: www.facebook.com/saminaraihealer

From Stepford Wife to Beauty Queen

By Teana Lynne

'It's never too late to be what you might have been.'
~ George Elliot

'Come and sit on my lap baby. Come and tell me what the matter is,' said my husband—my groomer and abuser. I felt sick. The colour drained from my face. The last place in the world I wanted to be was in this room, right now, with him, let alone sit on his lap. But I knew I had to. I had no choice.

I met him when I was fourteen. He was my school friend's dad, thirty-two years my senior. He seemed so lovely, so kind, thoughtful, generous, understanding, and open—the perfect dad to a fourteen-year-old. At times, I secretly wished my strict Victorian-style dad was more like him as he was so different.

Being an innocent, naive, ex-convent school educated girl, and a late developer with no self-confidence and little self-esteem, I didn't realise that he had obviously planned to manipulate me all along and was in it for the long game.

I realise now that he groomed me, before convincing me to move in when I was seventeen. I mean, what teenager wouldn't jump at the chance of supposed freedom, with no rent or bills to pay and the opportunity to live as the grown-up we think we are at that age?

Unfortunately, he did have a plan. After convincing me to dump my boyfriend—a nice young man my own age (the type your parents approve of)—he convinced me not to go to university. He told me I'd likely hate it and drop out as I was so mature for my age, guilting me into believing that I'd leave my parents in debt. Knowing life was often a struggle for them financially, I didn't go through with the plans I'd always dreamt of.

My mum used to call him Svengali. She was right, of course, although I didn't see it at the time. He brainwashed me. He gradually alienated and isolated me from friends; I didn't speak to my parents for the first six months after moving in with him because I thought they didn't understand me. This narcissistic sociopath love-bombed me until I hung onto his every word ... until I was trauma-bonded. I became completely dependent on him, financially and emotionally.

In my teens, I went to a camera club with a friend which boosted my confidence a little, giving me the dream of becoming a model. I even signed with an agency in Liverpool and did some great jobs including for a former shopping channel. I once got to kiss a model 'husband', a

Brad Pitt lookalike modelling wedding gifts. I was a finalist in a national modelling competition—'Vision in White'—which resulted in me being approached by a few London photographers.

This didn't fit his plan.

He convinced me they were charlatans and out to scam me. My dreams didn't count. So, they ended.

He controlled my every move, where I went. My only friends were his. He even controlled what I wore down to my lingerie, insisting on stockings and suspenders every day. I wasn't allowed to wear jeans or trousers and cover up my 'pretty legs', but was expected to dress up in skirts, blouses and high heels, even when going food shopping or doing housework. Tying my hair back or tucking it behind my ears wasn't allowed because 'it's prettier down'. I can still apply lip liner without a mirror to this day, after his constant 'your lippy needs fixing'. I was like a Stepford wife. Perfect to the outside world. But like a robot on the inside.

First, I was passed around his friends. Then, he trafficked me. This was my life.

I believed I'd made my bed and had to lie in it. I couldn't go back home. I believed this was my world.

I married him, believing his promises of a normal life. It broke my mum's heart. It was all part of his plan to control me, so I felt trapped. I was now legally his; his commodity to do with as he wished. He told me he owned me, he'd created me, so he could destroy me—I'd only ever leave dead in a box. Who would believe me if I dared to tell the truth? He played the charming husband with his public face. And I wore my 'mask'.

Some days, it wasn't that bad. Some clients were nicer than he was to me. They treated me with respect and were genuinely kind. One took me to Paris, another to New York. Then there were the times I was terrified. When I found a gun under the pillow. When I woke up in different clothes and no underwear, having been drugged. The days before mobile phones. I'm sure I had been raped, or at least sexually assaulted, but he didn't care. It was my fault for being stupid enough for accepting a cup of tea.

He never physically hurt me, which would be damaging the goods, but sexually I was his to objectify. To abuse. To use. I was his 'whore' and expected to perform like some actress from whatever sick, twisted porn film he chose.

He mentally and emotionally abused me. I was completely dependent on him, trauma-bonded, and I didn't even know who I was anymore.

At age thirty, I met a client who was charming, kind, well-to-do and treated me like a princess. Somehow, he gave me a spark of self-belief, spoiling me, treating me with respect, showing me off, taking me out—he even took me to Ibiza (albeit as his 'high-class escort').

I believed I had no way out and my husband—my groomer—would never let me go. I was worth too much financially. I believed he'd rather kill or disfigure me than let me go. I knew he was more than capable.

So, that day when he asked me to sit on his lap, I decided this was my moment. The time to be brave, braver than I had ever been before, and to be honest. I couldn't bear this life anymore. I thought I'd rather be dead than stay another day. I was terrified as I told him I didn't want to be with him anymore. I'd seen another life, another way, and I desperately wanted to be normal.

He lifted me off his lap and walked out. *This is it,* I thought, *the last day of my life*. I silently said goodbye to my parents, my life. I stood frozen for what felt like eternity.

He returned, telling me to pack my things in bin bags, and dragged my jewellery off me. He told me I could leave, but that there would be rules. I didn't care. I was going to be free. I couldn't believe it and didn't wait a second for him to change his mind.

I was dropped miles away in Chester, outside the client's apartment who had taken me to Ibiza, with thirteen years of life in bin bags, a ten-thousand-pound credit card debt he'd signed me up to, plus six hundred pounds that I'd managed to squirrel away. His rules included that I would always be his; I wasn't allowed to divorce him, he was entitled to his conjugal rights, and I was never to discuss him or our life. He played me a film, proving that he'd secretly filmed me, telling me there were duplicate copies, threatening to blackmail me if I broke his rules. I didn't care. I just wanted to be free, away from him. I'd worry about that later.

I went back once for some personal belongings he promised, sentimental stuff. He had burned my diaries I'd kept since I was twelve, obviously scared they were incriminating. I wore trousers, my hair tied up. As I nervously tried to leave, he quietly said, 'We can do it the nice way or the nasty way, now get up the fucking stairs!' He didn't stop despite my pleas or tears. He raped me. Cold-hearted and ruthless, he simply told me to wear stockings 'next time'.

This was the day I finally saw him for the evil sociopath he was.

It took me two years to get my divorce. The judge approved without his agreement as he refused to sign. Best revenge ever!

I finally told my partner that I'd been raped. He said he'd guessed but hadn't ever asked me about it. Why hadn't he convinced me to go to the police? I realise now that he too was a narcissist and was using me for his own benefit. I wasn't the first 'working girl' he had 'saved'.

At first, he was charming, love-bombing me, creating a fake romantic story of how we met, and convincing me it was better for me to hide my past—heaping on the shame instead of suggesting therapy and support. He financially supported me, his friends were my friends, and I was completely dependent on him, grateful for him saving me.

Don't get me wrong, he was nowhere near as bad as my groomer and trafficker. He just wanted me for his own sexual deviances and pleasure, using his knowledge of my past, my vulnerability, and my susceptibility to manipulate me into doing his bidding.

During this time, I met a woman who I fell for. It was a crazy, passionate three-month long affair with his encouragement, which wasn't healthy or normal. She opened my eyes. She reminded me that, although he might have saved me once, I deserved to live the life I wanted. I deserved my own dreams, and I shouldn't stay with him out of guilt or gratitude.

I followed the steps I had taken before, realising this wasn’t normal.

I tried to help with the cash flow problem he claimed to have, transferring debt to my perfect credit file. We lived our life on my cards, which he paid monthly (not in full, mind, just the minimum). We downsized our home to release equity to get clear, although I found out after I left that he owed more than three hundred thousand pounds on a two hundred-thousand-pound property. I discovered that he hadn’t paid the mortgage or his credit cards for two years!

I started to find my voice and began setting boundaries. As his drug use increased, so did his proclivity for associating with escorts and pimps. His ‘eccentric’ behaviour worsened from wearing nail polish to wearing high-heeled 'dominatrix' boots, introducing ‘escorts’ as his girlfriend and me as his wife. He invited random women to our home, expecting me to sleep with them, then calling me selfish when I refused. I raised my concerns over his escalating drug problem, but he denied that it was an issue.

Desperate for change, and his behaviour growing more erratic, I moved into the spare room to give myself space to think. I booked a break away with a friend to consider my choices. She stayed at our home as we had an early flight. He called the police demanding that she left his property. That was the last nail in the coffin. I could have saved the price of a holiday. I was done.

This time, I escaped with thirty-six thousand pounds of debt and my life in bin bags yet again. Aged thirty-eight, I moved into a room in a shared house to start again. From zero.

This is when my life really started. When I took back control.

I began to rebuild my confidence, my self-esteem and my sense of self. I started to become the real me. I experimented and tried new things.

I started to believe in myself. I'd left my previous job as a travel agent because the hours were inconvenient to my new man, my 'saviour', despite only training in this job after meeting him. I decided to put my career first and pushed myself in my corporate banking job, a job I had taken not long after I had married him. I was promoted several times over the next few years in what had been, in his words, a 'pocket-money job'.

I started a new relationship and, while it was not without its issues, we worked through it. It wasn't always a fairy tale and we split up a few times, both carrying 'baggage' from our pasts and needing time to heal. But we worked on it together, supporting one another, being each other's cheerleader.

I started to face my past, my shame and my guilt, and heal from it. With the help of my now fiancé, I realised it wasn't my fault. These things happened to me but did not define me.

I started to share my story, albeit at first from a victim mentality—in tears, certain people would shun me. Over time, I grew stronger and started to move to a survivor mentality. I never had counselling, I just learned to share openly. With time, I realised I had nothing to feel shame for. I watched the soaps, one depicting a grooming story and one depicting a story of control in a marriage, which helped me heal the most.

On a whim, harking back to my forgotten dream of becoming a model, I responded to an advert for a casting for a fashion show. I never expected a call-back, but got one! So, at age forty-seven, alongside women fifteen years (and more) my junior, I modelled for their social media marketing at instore fashion events, charity fashion shows, and finally their huge annual fashion event at Chester Racecourse.

With my self-belief growing, I started to prepare a portfolio, registered for an online modelling platform, and saw a casting for a modelling competition for the over forty-fives. With my fiancé's support, I decided *what the hell* and entered.

Initially, the competition was online due to the pandemic. To my delight I won a finalist's place and the title of Classic Miss Cheshire. Nine months later, aged forty-nine, I stood on stage alongside forty-nine other women and, to my absolute astonishment and joy, I won! I was crowned Classic Miss British Isles. I achieved my dream of winning a modelling contract.

That was it, I wanted more. I didn't want to be just a number in a big corporate business. I wanted to find my purpose in life. I'd reignited my passion and now I wanted to follow it. So, despite being at risk of redundancy for almost two years, clinging on with gritted teeth in a temporary role for eighteen months, I took the leap of faith and gave in my notice. On 31st January 2022, I left my 'secure' fifteen-year corporate career behind.

I'd spent the previous year learning about branding, social media marketing, copywriting, visibility, networking, and surrounding myself with the right community as I searched for my true purpose in life. I set up my business—Pathway to Potential—as the Model Mindset Mentor.

I am now living the life I was meant to.

I'm living my passion as a signed, published model, alongside my purpose of helping women just like me to rebuild their confidence, self-esteem and sense of self, so that they can fulfil their potential and achieve their dreams, just like I have. And this is just the beginning… .

If I can do it, so can you!

About the Author

Teana Lynne is a mature model, winner of Classic Miss British Isles 2021, and a confidence coach. Known as the 'Model Mindset Mentor', Teana discovered her passion late in life, having worked in corporate banking for nigh on fifteen years, but knowing in her heart she wanted to strike out on her own and do something more meaningful. With a traumatic past—having been the victim of grooming and sex trafficking, surviving two narcissistic relationships, overcoming 36k debt, starting from scratch (not just once but twice at age thirty and again at age thirty-eight); going from her life in binbags to owning her own home, building a successful career, rebuilding her confidence, self-esteem and sense of self—Teana is proof that you are never too old to start again and that dreams really *can* come true if you believe in yourself.

Connect with Teana:

Website: www.linktr.ee/Teana_Lynne

Life Isn't Perfect

By Tracey Toulmin

'Don't walk in front of me … I may not follow, don't walk behind me … I may not lead, just walk beside me … and be my friend!'
~ Albert Camus

The day I received the call will stay with me like a nightmare I can't wake from.

'Tracey, your daughter is scared of you. She says, "When Mummy is really angry and screaming, I feel scared."'

I too felt scared; scared of what might happen if I ever crossed the line, unable to control myself.

I stood outside work, the sun shining down on me, feeling frozen. Cold and glued to the spot, tears streamed down my face. *What do I do now? How do I even register that my daughter, in her second year of school, is scared of me?* The sadness rose; disappointment and anger at myself for letting it get this far.

I felt sick. How could I go back into the office, the dark space where I had no voice and was made to feel totally worthless? Now, at a time when I thought I could rely on my husband to tell me everything would be ok, I had to go back into the office feeling heartbroken. I tried to get back to work, but it was no good. I had to do something ... but what? What could I do to change how my colleagues perceived me and, most importantly, be the best mum I could and not have my daughter feeling the way she did?

That day, I not only felt worthless at work, but I now felt worthless at home, as a mum and a wife. Home was supposed to be my sanctuary, my place of happiness. The reality, however, was very different. I felt like a single parent, struggling with an independent young lady.

I left work emotionally 'broken' and somehow drove the short journey to the doctors' surgery, the winding roads seemingly going on forever.

Turning into the car park I noticed how full it was. *Damn, that plain waiting room, so quiet you could hear a pin drop, is going to be so full. I hope there isn't anyone I know waiting.*

I stood in a long queue, waiting to speak to the receptionist, feeling desperate and hopeless. Something within me was pushing me to break this cycle. I needed to do something to help my daughter and me feel safe. I knew that questions were going to be asked and overheard by the waiting patients but by this point I didn't care—I couldn't go on like this. I stood shaking, the sun beaming through the open windows. What was I going to say? *First ... second ... third person ... it's me next....* My heart pounded so much I thought everyone could hear it. *Keep calm, you'll be ok,* I kept telling myself.

Oh no, it's my turn. Shit, what am I going to say?

The receptionist looked up (with a look of impatience), 'Yes?'

Upon making eye contact I thought she could see my heart breaking. I squealed, almost collapsing at the desk, tears running down my face. The receptionist turned out to be the sweetest lady, promptly leading me through to a private room where I sat for what seemed like an eternity.

I could hear comings and goings, doors opening and closing. There I sat, sobbing in this little room, not knowing what I was going to do or say to whomever came to see me.

After a long time (and starting to panic because I would need to collect my daughter from nursery), a doctor called me through. Everywhere was so much quieter than when I had arrived. The doctor's room was cool. Before I sat down, I began to sob again. The doctor turned to me, speaking softly, and asked what had happened.

After a long conversation about how I felt at work and home, the doctor recommended that I restarted my medication and added me to the list to see a counsellor. I'm not quite sure how I felt when I left the doctor's, or what was actually said (even now, it is all a bit of a blur). I do recall thinking, *the tablets helped me last time, and I can come off them again when I feel ok … can't I?*

You see, I had been prescribed citalopram after losing my dad. I stopped taking them when I discovered I was pregnant. I thought I was ok without the medication, but the truth is, I wasn't. Most people I knew had no idea that I was struggling. I hid behind a mask. When I did trust and confide in others, it seemed to backfire; my mental health was used against me. When things happened at work it was blamed on what I was going through. This upset and frustrated me—my work was always done to the best of my ability. Family life became difficult because I would take my work problems home and would have no patience for my daughter or husband. We argued daily over silly things.

Between my husband and I, we worked long hours. He commuted to London and would leave before we woke up and did not return until our daughter was in bed. I felt like a single parent. I felt lonely and would snap at her. I did not like the angry person I had become.

So, *that* call was my wake-up call. Something had to change.

As the medication started kicking in, my counselling sessions began. I'd had sessions before and so was happy to attend, however, I worried that when they'd end, and I wouldn't feel any better. The six-week courses I'd had before never seemed enough; it would take that long just to start opening up and unravelling the madness going on inside my head. These days, I often say I could do with a pensieve like the one Dumbledore has in Harry Potter!

You might wonder, *why be open to it if it hadn't worked previously?* The first time, the counselling ended before issues were resolved. Also, I was aware that there was no connection between my counsellor and me—it can be difficult to open up if the vibration between you isn't right. This time, however, I knew I had to push through it. I had to get answers and results for me to move forward. This time *had* to be right.

The counsellor was a redhead, softly spoken and wore glasses. I thought her dress sense was a little quirky, always bright and cheerful. Her manner was so lovely and, from the beginning, she said she thought our time together was important and acknowledged that it may not be enough. We met once every two weeks at the doctors' surgery.

This counselling was different. I felt a shift. The counsellor seemed to understand me and my ways. We had a connection that I had never felt before; I felt at ease and could be more open. We had extra sessions—she said she felt I needed them. Before we parted company, she gave me details to apply for a free counselling service in our area. The forms were completed, which was quite difficult putting all my feelings of anger and sadness onto paper.

One question made me feel sick to the stomach to admit: have you ever considered taking your own life? *What do I put? Do I tell the truth, or do I lie?* 'YES', I responded, guiltily. Admitting this was hard, as is opening up to you today. It is not something my family or friends are fully aware of. By now, my husband was noticing a change in me—I was laughing more, calmer, and different around our daughter. He knew that this additional counselling would be beneficial.

Work was still horrid. I hated going in each day, but I gave everything, even though I felt worthless doing all the hard work that others weren't completing and taking the flak for their failings. Most of the people I worked with were amazing and I have some long-time friends who were there for me when I needed to vent; they could see what was happening but were powerless to help or act. Before leaving school, it was never my ambition to be an office worker and perhaps that's why it never suited me.

A letter finally arrived, arranging a telephone appointment; the gentleman was so lovely, but he said there was an eight-week wait for counselling. Feeling a little down-hearted and sobbing, I shared this news with my husband. I felt that all the work I had already done would be wasted. However, we kept talking to each other and working on our relationship (because that was important too).

In early autumn, I got a call saying that the counselling service had a slot for me—fantastic news!

The first appointment arrived. I stood outside at the back entrance to a doctors' surgery in the next town from where we lived. It was dark with only the distant sound of sports being played on the hill above the surgery. The car park was small and dimly lit. I hadn't parked there as

I missed the turning, worrying I was late or wouldn't be able to find it, so I had to walk from a side road in town. It was quite a trek, but it gave me time to think and feel calmer about meeting another counsellor.

A lady came to the door, her long wavy hair framing her polite looking face. She was so lovely and gently spoken, leading me through the bright corridor to her room. In the room there was a small desk, two chairs, a small table and a box of tissues. From the window behind her I could see people's legs walking by on the high street (I used to concentrate on these if I was struggling during a session).

We sat opposite each other. She asked me about myself, waiting until I was ready to say the things I needed to say. During some sessions I would blurt everything out that was happening at work and that would take most of the session; however, she would stop me and gently remind me why I was there.

All sorts of things came up and, for once, I was able to go back and gain closure for things that had happened as a child, as a teenager and as an adult—there were plenty of tears! I was the youngest of three and always felt that I got a raw deal and felt blamed for everything. Now, I feel at peace about my past.

I talked mostly about work and how people didn't understand me. For some reason I was angry at the world and at others who didn't have the same work ethic as me. You see, in my head there was a perfect world and a way that things are done. I'm still a little bit like this but I've learnt to be at ease with others' ways.

Often, I said, 'Is it me or is the world simply not perfect?'

The counsellor would say, 'Tracey, you have to realise you can't change other people's imperfections. In your head there is a perfect world … it doesn't exist.'

My husband was so understanding when I returned home after the sessions. I know that none of it was easy for him either, seeing his wife so vulnerable. I couldn't talk to him some evenings and would go straight to bed.

The sessions lasted for about a year. In fact, they only ended because we moved to North Wales. I wasn't ready for the sessions to end but life was changing. For the first time, I had been presented with someone—a counsellor—who got me and knew how to get the best side of me to show up. Her words still ring in my head today as I sit here writing my chapter on May's full moon—the Flower Moon (2022).

The thing is, it's not about changing others; it's about working on ourselves and realising that, while the world is not perfect, we can change how we are and how we feel.

After all those years of heartache and being angry I now live a much better-balanced life, continually working on my mind, body and soul and raising my energy and positivity to flow more naturally. I have learnt to be grateful each day for what I have; my husband and I laugh every day, and I look forward to each day with excitement of how things can truly be, even after feeling like you have hit rock bottom. Back in my old corporate life I was often asked where I want to be in five years. I never knew the answer then … but I do now.

Our dream came true to run our own business and reconnect as a family again—with love and laughter.

My husband and I have said that if we hadn't moved to Wales then we may not still be together. That would be a great shame because we bounce off one another. Each and every day is different, with plenty of laughs at Toulmin Towers. Living by the sea is amazing—if only we had done it sooner! Or maybe not because all that has happened was for a reason and that reason is right here, right now.

Life isn't perfect, it's what we choose to make it, and that comes with being open to possibilities that are there for us to take as they already exist for us.

Counselling helped me realise that I had to help *me* first.

About the Author

Tracey Toulmin is a four-star guest house owner with her family. She is wife to Joel, mum to her daughter and dog mum to Flash, who came to her when she lost her mum in 2018. Tracey believes Flash helped with her grief and continues to bring her through the dark moments.

When the pandemic hit in 2020, Tracey took to sharing her morning rambles on Facebook Live, showing where she lives and helping others to feel less alone. Since then, she has become a volunteer radio presenter for the local radio station, sharing her love of music and keeping jiggy on a Saturday morning.

Tracey believes sharing her story will help at least one person to be open to opportunities, which in turn can help another and so on.

Connect with Tracey:

Facebook: @tracey.toulmin.1 or @BrynWoodlandsHouse

Instagram: @brynwoodlandshouse

Website: www.brynwoodlandshouse.co.uk

Afraid of the Stigma

By Joanne Hughes

'Vulnerability is the only bridge to connection.' ~ *Brené Brown*

I woke up to a call bell going off and the sound of a baby crying. I rolled onto my side to see a clear crib, a baby with a mop of dark brown hair and red chubby cheeks wriggling inside. I remember questioning, *Is she mine?* She was beautiful.

Two days prior—two weeks past my due date—I had arrived at the hospital with my partner. My maternity bag was packed with lush goodies—I wanted a nice bath bomb and massage after my labour. My mum had always told me that it was like shelling peas. 'It's easy girl, you would have experienced worse period pains.' She had nearly delivered me in the back of a taxi, which I believe was only a twenty-minute drive to the hospital. I had attended all the anti-natal classes and was under the impression it would all go tickety boo … how naïve could I be?!

I was almost thirty-three and considered myself to be pretty clued up. I had an established career, travelled a little and had bought my own home. I had lived independently for years. I'd had a few relationships but had never been ready to settle down until I met my husband. When I found out I was pregnant, I felt immense joy and apprehension. I didn't particularly enjoy my pregnancy. The early excitement of showing off my little bump was quickly replaced with worry. I couldn't wait for my pregnancy to be over and for the safe arrival of our daughter.

At the hospital, I was taken down to the labour ward to be induced. The midwife shared the same name as me—'Jo'. She was newly qualified but appeared to be very competent and had a lovely manner about her. I remember feeling at ease and thinking, *I can get through this*. My labour had slowed down and I was given the syntocinon IV drip to speed up my contractions. I remember watching This Morning with Phil and Fern. I'd never been a fan, but I thought concentrating on the television would help to distract me from the contractions. Unfortunately, Jo would leave me in a few hours when her shift ended. She was replaced by another midwife, who was friendly and professional, but I didn't feel the same rapport. My husband was trying his best to support me but, in that moment, I needed to feel that I could trust the midwife. When she mentioned that it was her first shift back after maternity leave, it was like music to my ears. She had recently given birth—she understood! It didn't matter to me that the previous midwife hadn't gone through labour, but I felt vulnerable and needed to make a connection. The contractions got stronger and more frequent, and I welcomed a dose of pethidine. Although it didn't get me much further on in my labour, it took the pain away for a while. It took away my anxiety—for a while, I didn't care!

It was shift changeover and my third midwife introduced herself. She checked how far dilated I was and in a very abrupt manner said, 'You'll be here for a while longer yet!' I felt like it was my fault that my labour had slowed down. Had I been doing something wrong? The atmosphere in the room had been upbeat until now. I explained that I felt worried about the length of time I had been in labour and the potential physical impact on my baby. When the midwife rolled her eyes, it was the final straw. I asked to speak to the doctor who agreed my labour had gone on long enough. I was absolutely exhausted by this point. My daughter was delivered in theatre via episiotomy. I recognised one of the theatre nurses. Ironically, I had stood in the same theatre with him five years back, when I had witnessed a caesarean section as a student nurse. He had laughed as I'd nearly fainted! And now, here I was, my legs in stirrups for all to see. I'd got to a point where I didn't care or give it a second thought (until I was sat opposite him on a mandatory training course almost a year later).

My baby and I were kept in hospital for a few days as I had needed a blood transfusion. I enjoyed this time with my girl, chatting to the other mums.

I had been home a couple of days when I started experiencing intense anxiety. I was worried that I couldn't cope and started worrying about dropping my baby. I was experiencing intrusive thoughts and, although in a professional capacity I could spot the signs in someone else, I was unable to recognise them in myself. I would avoid carrying my baby up or downstairs and use the excuse that I felt dizzy due to low iron. I had been discharged with iron tablets, so this seemed plausible. One night, these thoughts were so intense I called my husband home from work, using the excuse that I felt physically unwell. At the time, I couldn't share my thoughts and feelings with him because I was afraid that he would think I wasn't good enough to be a mum to our daughter. In fact, that's exactly how I felt—not good enough!

I dreaded the first meeting with the health visitor. When she came, I was surprised at how easy going she appeared. I think I was expecting the old stereotypical stern health visitor who would tell me I was doing everything wrong. Even though she told me that I was doing a great job and how my daughter was reaching her predicted milestones, I really didn't believe it. During one visit, I wanted to tell her how I was feeling, but then I didn't know if I was making something out of nothing. I was asked to complete a questionnaire to assess my mood, the same questionnaire I had completed many times with patients. My husband, being his jovial self, was telling a joke which the health visitor found hilarious. I would have found the joke hilarious myself only I was struggling to see the funny side of anything. I pretended to laugh and completed the questionnaire as if I were ok—I didn't want to bring the mood down.

I felt so isolated, and this was compounded when I was invited out for a walk with one of the mums I had befriended on the ward. I really didn't want to leave the house but made the effort. I kept telling myself that I had to do it for my daughter. We met in a park close to my house. It was the first time I had been out by myself without my husband. During our walk we caught up with how life had been since being discharged from the labour ward. I remember her saying that she felt so content and fulfilled since having her daughter. All I could think was how empty I felt and terribly guilty for feeling this way. I didn't venture out with my daughter for a while afterwards.

I eventually attended a mother and baby session at the local health centre. As usual, I pretended that I was coping with motherhood and actually enjoying it. I wasn't brave enough to say that I wasn't coping mentally. On the surface, everything appeared well. My daughter looked well cared for. In fact, she was well cared for, I just didn't believe it. Being a mental health nurse, I was afraid that others would judge me. If I shared that I wasn't coping emotionally and mentally then I wouldn't be fit to work with people with mental health problems.

I continued to go through the motions as I had a wedding to organise. My partner and I had planned to get married in the August before I returned to work. It was stressful but also a distraction to how I was feeling. My anxiety around motherhood improved, although I still didn't entirely believe that I was good enough at it. Our big day came and, looking back, my mood was still flat. I had looked forward to this day whilst I was pregnant. It was supposed to be the second most special day after having our daughter—the day we officially became a family—but I felt flat. I put on a front that I was having a great time and I felt such relief when the day was over, and everyone started disappearing to their rooms.

When my daughter was almost seven months old, I returned to work as a community mental health nurse. Where some women are besides themselves with sadness at the end of their maternity leave, all I could feel was relief. There was never any doubt that I didn't love my daughter deeply, but I was overwhelmed with the responsibility of looking after her. I went back to work full-time, and my daughter had a place in nursery. The nursery staff were amazing, especially Aunty Debbie, who never said anything, but could tell I was struggling so offered gentle guidance and advice. I completely trusted the nursery and my daughter thrived there. My mood started to improve, and when my daughter was almost a year old, I started to feel like I was doing an OK job as her mum.

My daughter was fourteen months old when I found out I was pregnant again. I wasn't as anxious during this pregnancy, but following the birth of my second daughter, my anxiety returned. I felt exhausted! I think the lack of rest and overwhelm of having a newborn and a toddler to look after had contributed to the decline in my mental state (although I don't think I fully recovered after having my first born—I had just learnt to mask it). I started having intrusive thoughts that my daughter was going to choke to death whilst in my care. The feelings were so intense that I would make sure that my phone was unlocked and within arm's length whilst feeding her. I don't know where this fear came from. It wasn't as if my eldest daughter had ever choked whilst weaning. It was completely irrational, but the fear of her choking had stopped me from giving my youngest baby solid food. Fortunately, the health visitor (a different one this time) picked up on this.

I attended the clinic with my baby girl, and I was handed the same questionnaire as before to assess my mood. I made sure that I scored low but without it looking like I was trying to cover something up. When she challenged me and said, 'It's ok not to be ok you know!' I burst into tears. I had to admit to myself that I was struggling, and I felt guilty. Why was I feeling so sad when I was so lucky to have two beautiful girls? I recognise now that my feelings of guilt was part of my depression. The health visitor knew I was a mental health nurse and had a frank discussion about how antidepressant medication could help my anxiety and depression. I was reluctant to take medication, even though I had advised patients about the benefits of antidepressants on many occasions. I just couldn't recognise how this would benefit my mental state. I wasn't sure I was depressed—I felt sad much of the time—but depressed? I knew I worried about my baby choking but also felt that, if I stopped worrying and took my eye off the ball, it would happen. I was stuck in a cycle of unhelpful thinking but couldn't see it.

When my health visitor mentioned a referral to the primary care mental health team, I felt sick. There was no way I could have my referral read out in front of colleagues. I worked for the assertive outreach team and a representative from each team would attend the referrals meeting every Monday morning. I had attended that meeting on many occasions. I felt cold at the thought of colleagues knowing that I couldn't cope with motherhood—how could I return to work from maternity leave with them knowing that I had needed to access services? Looking back, I was petrified of the stigma attached to having mental health problems and how this would influence how others viewed me as a mental health nurse. I think this stemmed from when I first qualified and started working on an inpatient unit. Staff who openly struggled with their mental health were viewed as weak and not fit to do the job. It was more acceptable to drink excessively every night than it was to admit to taking antidepressant medication.

It wasn't until I was having my third child that I addressed my mental health issues. I was working as an eating disorder practitioner and, although I had not personally experienced having an eating disorder, during the assessments and therapy sessions the patients' experiences were resonating with me. Even though I no longer worked within mental health services in my local area, I still felt vulnerable accessing them from the other side. I sourced private therapy and started attending weekly sessions. I started to address the underlying issues that were driving my mental health problems. I was probably hell to live with for a few months, but it was the best investment I have ever made in myself and for my family. I was thankful that my husband was so supportive and understanding. When my son was born, I was able to enjoy every early milestone with him. I remember watching him chomping on a carrot, with a smile on his chubby face, thinking how far I had come. I attended the mother and baby groups and made friends that I still have to this day.

Having a baby is a stressful life event, whether you're a new mum or not. The more I exposed myself to groups and social events, the more I found mums who were able to talk about their struggles which normalised my feelings of overwhelm. In turn, I hope sharing my experience helps you, too.

About the Author

Joanne Hughes is an aesthetics nurse and the owner of Simply Youthful Aesthetics, based in Llangollen, North Wales. A qualified mental health nurse since 2003, Joanne holds a part-time post within the NHS. She is also currently studying the non-medical prescribing course at Salford University to become an Independent Nurse Prescriber.

Joanne trained in aesthetics in November 2019, just before the pandemic hit, and was forced to close her doors only a couple of months later as the country went into lockdown. Through grit, determination and consistency, she has managed not only to keep her business afloat during a pandemic but has seen her business develop and grow. Joanne believes that showing up as her authentic self has enabled her to develop her ideal client base, who are ladies of a similar age - 47 years young, who want to look more youthful yet maintain a natural look.

Connect with Joanne:

Facebook: www.facebook.com/joannemarie1974

Instagram: www.Instagram.com/simplyyouthfulbyjoanne

She is so Loved ... Why is She so Wounded?

By Julie Buchanan

'Be kind, for everyone you meet is fighting a great battle.'
~ Philo of Alexandria

Marrying my soulmate, Iain, was truly one of the best days of my life. It was a dream come true. We had a beautiful celebration outside Brighton, surrounded by nature and sheep, celebrating with our family and friends. We both felt on top of the world. A few days later, we took a ten-day honeymoon to Mexico, embracing the culture, soaking up the sunshine, and enjoying every moment with each other—and what an amazing holiday we had!

A few weeks later, we found out we were pregnant—another dream of ours to come true. Excited and grateful, we were on top of the world.

It felt like a fairy tale. Our twelve-week scan came, and we could hear the first heartbeat of our baby, a truly emotional moment. We were so happy. Then, our twenty-week scan arrived ... the beginning of life testing us. In the scan room, the first lady was really quiet while scanning the bump. My husband and I could feel some hesitations about our baby girl developing differently. Two more ladies came to check the scan and confirmed that we needed to get some further checks on the anatomy and growth of our baby.

We were referred to a consultant who informed us that our baby had her stomach and liver reversed and he was referring us to further consultants at King's College, London. After leaving this first consultation, I thought how lucky we were to be so well looked after. In September 2015, we took our first trip to London. We both felt anxious, unsure what to expect. On arrival at the hospital, we were guided to our first appointment with the heart consultant. *Heart?!* At this point, I could feel the shock setting in. We entered the consultancy room where three consultants were waiting. One of the consultants began to talk about our baby girl's heart. By now, I was trying to keep myself together as I wasn't sure how to handle the information. In a nutshell, the consultant explained that the heart of our baby had formed differently. She had two left atriums instead of a left and a right, and a missing tube. Somehow, however, the heartbeats were (so far) working perfectly. After this first appointment, I remember feeling so much pain. Sat in the waiting room,

tears had started to flood—I couldn't contain my emotions.

I pulled myself together to meet our next consultant, an expert on the stomach. This next appointment was overwhelming. I was being scanned while surrounded by a few professors who were interested in investigating the anatomical development of my baby. They were curious about how my baby was developing but were unsure how (or if) she would survive. I was asked if I still wanted to go ahead with the pregnancy as no one was sure of the outcome. I didn't need to think twice. I was so connected with my bump, and my baby girl was so wanted, that I firmly said, "Yes, I want to bring my baby girl into the world."

After spending five hours in the hospital that day, going through all those consultations and travelling back on the train, my husband and I felt numb, exhausted and drained. A mix of hope and anxiety were hanging in the air. At that time in my life, I had eight years' experience as a holistic therapist and qualified Reiki Master healer. Whether it was the tools I had, the love that I was receiving from my family and friends, or my sheer determination to manifest a healthy baby girl (even though, with four months of pregnancy ahead, I didn't know if she would survive), I made a choice: I chose to believe that I would manifest the chance to see my baby girl alive.

Over the next four months, my selfcare became my priority. I made sure that I rested when my body needed it, and I received regular massage and healing. My favourite time of the day was in the evening when I could put my feet up; I was massaging all day at the time which involved lots of standing on my feet. In the evening, as soon as I started to put my feet up so that I could spend time connecting with the bump,

I could feel her kicking me with a cheerful vitality that always filled me with hope and gratitude.

At eight months pregnant, I received regular check-ups with the midwives and was able to listen to my baby girl's heartbeat regularly, which always made me feel emotional and happy at the same time. I had to have a meeting with another consultant as there was a possibility that my baby would need surgery when she was born. The birth was coming close, and my anxiety was rising. At forty-two weeks, my baby hadn't arrived. After another check with the midwife, I was informed that I would be induced in two days if she didn't come before. Luckily, the contractions began, and we called a taxi to take us directly to the hospital. I remember the journey being a never ending, bumpy ride. But we arrived safely—another journey into the unknown.

The birth was laborious, traumatic and very long, but our baby girl arrived safely in January 2016. I managed to give her a kiss on her forehead before she was taken straight to the Neo-natal Intensive Care Unit (NICU). The pain was intense, not the physical pain, but the emotional pain that had engulfed my whole body. Being a first-time mum and having my baby taken straight away from my arms was distressing. Not being able to hold my baby in my arms, having carried her for nine months, was immensely difficult. I was lucky enough to be given a separate room, as my body not only needed healing emotionally but also physically. After a few hours of rest, my husband helped me to go and see our baby girl. I had to be pushed in a wheelchair as I wasn't able to walk. I carefully hugged my baby. Her tiny body was wrapped in so many tubes. I wished her goodnight, kissed her forehead, then headed back to my dedicated bedroom to rest for the night.

The following day was one of the most difficult of my life. My husband entered my room, a very sad, serious look in his eyes. He said, "We need to go and meet the surgeon. He wants to talk to us." My mind raced with so many questions and uncertainty. After my husband's words, I broke down. Tears came flooding, and I couldn't hold any back as I could feel what was coming. My two-day-old girl needed an operation to survive. I felt trapped in my worst nightmare, trying to see if I could wake up from what was happening. As we arrived in NICU, where my little girl was sleeping peacefully, a surgeon and consultant welcomed us into the room. I was given my baby to hold, then the surgeon introduced himself and very calmly explained what was happening. They had tried to pass a food dye through her tiny body but there was a blockage, and nothing was passing through. "We need to do an operation on your daughter," he said. Then he said something that will forever stay with me, a tool that I would go on to implement with my family, clients and mentoring programs: "I am not sure what I am going to find, I can't promise you the end result, but I AM GOING TO TRY." I hung onto those words for the four difficult hours of surgery that followed almost immediately after our meeting.

Surgery began at 8pm until midnight, when I received a call. I remember it so well. I was looking at my phone ringing and I could see that it was the hospital. I hesitated for a few moments, in fear of the news. On the phone, the surgeon's assistant told us that our baby girl had made it through, and she was fighting the tube in her mouth to be removed. From that day, I knew I had a warrior by my side.

The next morning, the doctors informed me that the healing process could take between two to six weeks before my baby was able to come home. I remember looking at the doctors straight in their eyes and defiantly declaring that my baby girl would be home in two weeks. I was desperate to take her home. It was even more difficult as, that day, my baby was waiting to be transferred from the baby unit to the children's hospital. I had to go home as they didn't have a bed for me for two nights. I remember going home, feeling numb—everything felt surreal. I couldn't wait for the next morning to come so that I could go back to the hospital and hold my baby in my arms. After a few days, my girl and I were settled into the children's hospital. Two weeks after her operation, we were told that we could all go home! It was such a beautiful moment for us as my parents had come to visit from France and were able to drive us all home together.

Coming home was our first success. We were so grateful to have finally started our journey as a family of three. From then on, lots of healing needed to take place. The first few months of being a new mum was difficult mentally. All the months of being strong while pregnant caught up with me and I had so many doubts. *Am I good enough? Am I a good mum? Am I a good wife?* The questions spun around my head until I made a choice: to turn my journey of becoming a mother into a journey of strength and resilience. I continued to do what was best for my family and me. We lived by the sea at the time so daily walks in fresh sea air had become our morning and afternoon ritual. We were surrounded by amazing friends who kept checking on how we were doing. I also kept working on my mindset by reading self-development books—learning has always been a passion of mine and so I wanted to keep myself as positive as possible to make sure my baby was getting the best of me. By making this decision to work on myself, to try my best day by day, I saw the ripple effect on the people surrounding me. When my daughter Amber reached the age of two, she finally got discharged by the surgeon with no more check-ups in the foreseeable future. It was such a beautiful celebration for the three of us and we decided to start a new chapter in our life.

We moved to a little village outside Chester, Cheshire. We arrived in February 2018, and in March 2018, I birthed my new business, The Amethyst Soul. This move has helped us to heal, find peace and rebuild ourselves. The journey of my pregnancy has been an intense roller coaster, but I am so thankful for all of it—it has shaped and strengthened me to help others through their pain. My daughter is six-and-a-half now and full of life with only a scar on her tummy. When she asks about her scar, I always tell her that a beautiful scar is what has kept her alive and to always be proud of it.

This experience has also deepened my healing practice. Going through emotional pain myself and being an empath has helped me to support my clients in the best way possible. I have always been soul-searching; like an artist, the need to learn and create has always been strong in me. My 'why' has always been to be of service to others and give back part of my soul to help others to follow their path within. So, alongside my practice as a well-being and Reiki practitioner, I have developed mentoring programs to help my clients step into their soul purpose.

I am a strong believer that every event that happens in your life is meant to propel you to get to know yourself better. As I continue on the journey of deepening my practice as a healer, I also have my little free spirit, Amber, by my side—my best teacher in life. You can always learn so much through pain; even in a negative situation you have a choice on how you respond.

Stay open to learn in any situation, whether it is pain or joy, as you can always turn it into magic. Each human is given a journey when they set their first foot on Earth; you can learn so much, every step of the way. This is only one part of my journey. I am truly grateful for the love I have received during this time, even if it has shaken me to the core of my soul…

But I know that this was part of the plan to step into my soul purpose.

About the Author

Julie Buchanan is an awakening healer, wellbeing practitioner and a Soul Purpose Mentor. She specialises in helping others to reconnect and realign their mind-body-soul so they can shine their light to the world.

Julie has fifteen years of experience in the massage and healing industry, where she has developed her unique signature treatments over the years. Her passion is helping others when they are in a dark place and helping them to work within so they can follow their truth and embrace their soul purpose.

Julie is based in Chester, Cheshire. You can also find Julie hosting and collaborating in awakening workshops and retreats across Wales and England.

Connect with Julie:

Website: www.theamethystsoul.com

Facebook: www.facebook.com/theamethystsoul

Instagram: www.instagram.com/the_amethyst_soul

I Was Alive But Not Living

By Heather Palfreyman

'You are not putting yourself first, you are putting yourself on the same level you put everyone else.' ~ Unknown

I had so much to be grateful for, but all I wanted to do in that moment was throw myself down the stairs…

I felt trapped, exhausted. I needed to escape.

I stood at the top of the stairs. It was midnight. My baby had woken again. Stood in my dressing gown, I thought, *what if … I just 'fell'?*

I needed to rest.

I needed a break.

I didn't want to keep on going like this, feeling this way, but I didn't know what to do.

Surely, I could do it in a way that I didn't kill myself? Just hurt myself enough so I could go to hospital for a few days and have a rest...

***

Motherhood was not the dreamy life I had envisioned. It was hard, tiring, and challenging. I found becoming a mum one of the toughest transitions ever. And whilst I absolutely love being a parent, even now I sometimes question if I am 'fit for the job'. But I am learning more about me, and what being a 'great mum' actually means to me.

I was never particularly maternal or gushy over newborn babies, and whenever I held one, they just cried. I didn't know how to be around babies or younger children, which is odd as I have three younger siblings.

But, as an ambitious, driven and motivated individual, I thought becoming a mum would be a piece of cake. I genuinely thought that the children would just fit into my life; I would be able to continue working my network marketing business and life would be hunky dory.

I absolutely loved being pregnant. I felt amazing, sexy. I had boobs, I glowed (most of the time) and I was in the best shape of my life. I did have scares with both pregnancies, and felt tired and lethargic at times, but I was so proud that I was able to 'make' these tiny humans, and that I was able to continue building my business.

I was so protective over my babies, and I still am to this day. I absolutely love my boys to bits, but gosh—parenting is tough!

2015

My first baby arrived, healthy and happy. I was overwhelmed and spent hours cuddling him, staring at him, and wondering how the hell he had gone from being in my tummy one moment, to in my arms the next. It was a miracle.

I struggled to breastfeed; I struggled with the lack of sleep, and the frustration of not being able to settle him. I remember going to a baby fair which was only a twenty-minute drive away just to have a break. I felt like a zombie and needed respite.

The following month was Mother's Day and I remember my husband getting me a card from my son and a beautiful frame with 'Mum' on it, with words of what a mother is. I felt like a fraud.

How does he know that? I thought. *He's only six weeks old, and he won't even breast feed. He doesn't love me. All he does is cry because he's hungry but when I feed him it just hurts, and he won't latch on properly. If I ask for help or give him a bottle, I'll be a failure! It's me that needs a bottle! A bottle of wine, but I can't even nip out to the shop to get one because he's upstairs in bed!*

I know now that I am not alone in these thoughts, so if you are feeling this way—you are not alone. Please reach out.

I didn't ask for help but, looking back, I am sure that I had postnatal depression (PND). I was scared to reach out in case they took my baby away. So, I carried on, doing my very best.

Things did get better, and I got into a new routine. I was on track in my business to qualify for another European weekend break, and we were on track to reach a significant promotion.

Life was amazing and, by this point, my baby did fit into our lives—rather nicely actually.

I felt so happy.

We went on lots of holidays, days out, had quality time together and made loads of amazing memories. I look back on those years with huge smiles, a warm heart and pride.

A year later, I was able to retire from the rat race at the age of thirty. This was one of my ultimate goals and I was so incredibly proud of myself for achieving this. I was able to contribute financially to family life more too … but still only able to pay for holidays and fun stuff. I wasn't yet in a position to pay half of the household bills—another goal I was chasing.

2017

Business was booming. I was speaking on stages and sharing my story with thousands of business partners across the UK about how I had built my business—initially around working three jobs, seven days a week, to being pregnant and then with my baby boy. I absolutely loved speaking on the stage and sharing my story and top tips so I could help others.

A major highlight was the talk I shared in June 2017, when I spoke on the same stage as 'Big Al'—a legend in the network marketing industry. I came ALIVE on that stage! My passion, my purpose and my mission were right there.

It was crystal clear (along with my vision for 2021) what I wanted to achieve.

A month later, we found out we were expecting our second child.

I was SO excited! I ran downstairs to share the news with my partner and nearly fell halfway down because I ran so fast.

I had a bleed a few weeks later and ended up having an early scan where it was confirmed that there were two embryos and one sac (twins). I had a complete mental breakdown at home a few days later—I didn't know how I would cope financially, mentally or emotionally.

I couldn't speak to anyone because we hadn't told anyone, and my husband simply said, 'Stay positive. We will be ok.' I ended up recording a video from the bath to myself, which I watched whilst writing this chapter and, my goodness, I wasn't in a good place. I felt alone, like a failure, weak, and I didn't even have the energy to pick my son up from nursery. I was at rock bottom with no way out. I never want anyone to feel like this. I was sobbing watching the video, but recording it really helped me at the time.

We ended up having vanishing twin syndrome, which I have never fully dealt with. I was just so relieved that we had one healthy baby.

I got myself back on track, back to business, and back to the happy, smiley, positive Heather that I was known for.

December 2017

I suffered my first ever panic attack at a leadership event I had qualified for. I was in a room full of achievers and superstars, and I felt incredibly overwhelmed. I was one of the youngest people in the room—I felt insane imposter syndrome. I was overcome with emotion and had to run to the toilets. I couldn't breathe, I couldn't stop crying—I lost control of myself.

That day, I sobbed my heart out. I didn't know what was wrong, and I tried to fight it, but my body was telling me to go home and rest.

I decided to take some time out and take maternity leave. I had four months to prepare for my second child and savour the moments and memories as a family of three.

2018

Four days before my due date, I was at my company's annual conference, and every new announcement I thought I was going to pop! Now, many people wouldn't have even considered going to the event but, as I've already mentioned, I'm incredibly ambitious and like taking risks.

I was so excited to bring my second son into the world. I had loved being pregnant and, two days before he was due, looked into hypno-birthing. I had seen that the 'Unmumsy Mum' had recently given birth, and hypno-birthing had helped her. I found a few freebies online and dived straight in whilst bouncing away on my ball. It was such an amazing tool and it helped me so much.

My son arrived safe and well on his actual due date—YES, I had achieved another goal!

I was so lucky. I had an amazing partner, two healthy boys and a loving family around me. I had worked my business and saved up enough money for my partner to take four weeks paternity which was amazing. It meant I would have some extra help and not feel like I did the first time round.

This time did feel a bit easier, and I was more willing to ask for help. I both breast and bottle fed which took so much pressure off me and meant my partner could also develop more of a bond and connection with our son. In the next few weeks, we also decided to get married the following year. Those four weeks of paternity leave soon went, and I was home alone again.

The next few months are a bit of a blur. I remember getting back to business and taking my baby with me, whilst also trying to be present for my toddler and plan a wedding.

That summer, my partner was in and out of hospital. It was an incredibly tough time for the whole family. It was all getting too much for me, but I had no choice but to continue pushing on. I felt like a swan—effortlessly gliding along but paddling like hell to keep it all together underneath.

I WAS EXHAUSTED!

I needed to rest.

I needed to sleep.

I needed a break.

I didn't know how I was going to get myself out of this nightmare. This monotonous cycle of waking up every day to try and make it through until bedtime.

I was in survival mode…

As I stood at the top of the stairs, frozen, I saw myself fall. Hitting my head as I went, I tumbled down the stairs—all thirteen of them—until I landed at the bottom. I was numb. I felt nothing.

Fortunately, that was all in my head, but the emptiness was real. I couldn't bring myself to slip. *What about my boys, my family—how would they cope without me here?*

Inside, I was screaming out for help but terrified to ask. I was yearning for someone to ask, 'How are you? How are you REALLY?' and for them to listen without judgement and say, 'I hear you, I understand, I'm here.'

I was so desperate for a break, but I felt pathetic. I was 'just tired', or at least that's what I had convinced myself.

I was so desperate that I had planned to throw myself down the stairs as a way to justify to others (and myself) that I needed a break.

I desperately wanted to be an amazing mummy, wife and businesswoman. I knew it was possible—there was proof all around me. But it just wasn't happening for me. Why?! I was working so hard and, whilst I was making progress, it wasn't happening quickly enough.

My family and friends offered to help, which I did accept and was incredibly grateful for, but I didn't feel I could rest or go to sleep. I felt so guilty that they would be looking after our children whilst I slept, and so I worked on my business instead.

I had a belief that an amazing mum had to have a spotless home, cook fresh meals every night, enjoy arts and crafts, and love absolutely every waking moment with her children—that is not the reality for most mums. (I talk about being a mum here because that's what I know. But I imagine being a parent in general is pretty tough and challenging at times.) This doesn't mean we love our children any less; merely acknowledging the lows as well as the highs.

For the next eighteen months or so, the universe kept throwing more challenges at me. It was the toughest and most challenging time of my entire life so far—I did not know how I was going to make it through.

In July 2020, at the height of the pandemic, I felt lost. I had no purpose and I felt like a total failure. I was a shouty, moody and stressed-out mum and business owner, and an angry and bitter wife, jealous that my husband got eight hours of respite at work each day while I had to juggle the business, home school and entertain the children during lockdown. We had recently moved house and I felt desperately lost and unfulfilled trying to look after the children, keep the house tidy and work my business in the evening when I was exhausted!

The life I was living was a far cry from the one I had dreamed of.

I was afraid of what my life looked like in the future. My youngest was starting school in 2022 and I had nothing for me—no hobbies, few friends and no social life. I only had my network marketing business. I had two choices: stay unhappy and unfulfilled or take some personal responsibility for my life and make some changes.

I wanted some friends who were like-minded and available for a mid-week pub lunch or walk in the park; people who were ambitious, driven and wanted more out of life, who really understood me, my crazy ideas and my entrepreneurial mindset.

Only, I had forgotten who Heather was… .

Remembering Me

I knew things needed to change. But I didn't know where to start. I was at rock bottom and needed support. But not from a counsellor (I had counselling and hated it—I wanted to look forward not dig up the past), or anyone I knew. I wanted to speak to someone who had been where I was, who understood where I was at, how I was feeling, and then help me move forward.

Things needed to change … and fast. If I carried on as I was, there was no way I would achieve my five-year vision to 'create a life where I am abundant in love, choices, time, money, relationships and health by the time I am thirty-five, if not before'.

I guess this is the first step to make changes—recognising where you are, that you aren't happy, and that YOU want to take action instead of (eventually) regretting living a life that was unfulfilled because you didn't put yourself on the same level as everyone else.

Not long after I had these thoughts, the Law of Attraction was at work. I saw a post in a Facebook group from a coach offering a free thirty-minute call. I was nervous as hell but got in touch because I was more scared of staying stuck where I was. I almost cancelled the call on the day; my self-doubt kicked in and I worried that I might get told to stop being silly and to crack on. But that call was the start of remembering who Heather was and stepping back into my power.

I was asked a few questions that made me think, *what is it that I do for me? What do I enjoy? What lights me up?* and I struggled to answer them. After a while I said, 'I love inspiring people, being on stage, sharing my top tips and helping others to live the life they truly desire.' And that was the start of finding me again.

I couldn't help others if I didn't first help myself. It was time to take some personal responsibility instead of blaming my circumstances and everyone else around me.

From Lost to Living My Best Life

In August 2020, I made my first big financial and time investment in me, and a business that I hadn't even started yet. It was scary, and I said no at first, continuing to find excuses ('it's not the right time', 'I haven't got the money'). I didn't think I was worthy, and I was scared that I might fail again. However, after my husband said, 'Go for it, I believe in you,' I went ahead. I felt sick, but excited too! My fire had been re-lit, my passion burned bright, and I took action.

I started to focus on Heather again.

I took small steps to start. I would take a fifteen-minute walk around the block alone. I took time to do my hair and put my make up on before I sorted the boys out, and even started buying myself a small bunch of flowers. I set goals for *me*… and that was the start of Heather being reborn and founding my very own company—More Than Just Mum® Coaching and Mentoring—in September 2020.

August 2022

My boys are four and seven, my partner is now my husband, and I have just booked my ninth holiday of the year (our next few holidays are booked too). I now pay my half of the household bills, which have significantly increased. I drive my dream car (which I had put in my first goal book in 2011) and I am able to invest back into my businesses (and me) every month, as well as having a career I absolutely adore! And I have an amazing network of friends and clients across the UK who all 'get' me.

I founded More Than Just Mum® because I wanted to help women who were just like me—ambitious, driven, motivated and wanting more from life but who felt stuck, lost, and needed guidance—to get back on track and remember who they are.

I get to help others put themselves on the same level they put everyone else, and to live their best lives—guilt free!

About the Author

Heather Palfreyman is a passionate, ambitious and rebellious goal getter! She's a multiple business owner and mum of two boys. Heather has been in the network-marketing industry since 2011, and in September 2020, she founded More Than Just Mum®—a coaching and mentoring business for women.

After her second child was born in 2018, Heather lost her purpose, felt stuck in a funk, and was barely surviving each day. After two and a half years of feeling alone, like a failure and at a total loss, she reached out to a coach, and remembered who she was and what she was passionate about. More Than Just Mum® was born.

Heather is now a highly sought-after goal setting, accountability and mindset coach for women in life and business, as well as a leader in her network-marketing business. She helps other women to start living their best life—guilt free!

Connect with Heather:

Website: www.HeatherPalfreyman.co.uk

Setting Fire to The Box

By Katie Felton

'Nothing can dim the light which shines from within.'
~ Maya Angelou

Life was all about boxes. Not physical storage boxes but emotional, societal, and self-imposed subconscious ones. Staying small in my box and not being 'too much'; looking a certain way, doing the right things, being what was expected. Feeling life was ruled by 'should': I *should* do this, *should* do that, *should* be a certain way … ticking off the list … ticking those boxes.

So, stepping off my high-flying career trajectory felt like another way to not tick the 'right' box. I felt I was disappointing people by making a choice for my health; to help the anxiety, to manage my endometriosis and the crippling pain that came with it. Choosing to remove stress and take a step for me felt like I was letting everyone down. And this feeling just kept coming… .

The one box I felt I should have been able to fulfil—giving my parents a grandchild, my husband a son or a daughter, becoming a mum—was one that I couldn't tick. Instead, it tore me apart, breaking me physically and emotionally. Our journey to become parents was a difficult one—something that isn't widely spoken about. So, when it was happening for us, it was a lonely and very isolated, desolate place.

We moved very quickly from the joy of impending parenthood, adjusting to the rapid changes happening to my body, to a place of grief and shock. I had a bit of bleeding, so went for a check-up scan. We saw our baby and heard their heartbeat. And, although they were the size of a legume, both fell madly in love. Room was made in my heart for them.

We were asked to go back a week later. 'Nothing to worry about,' they said. Sadly, that appointment went very differently. I was totally unprepared for it. I felt railroaded and blindsided.

When the second sonographer was asked into the room, we knew things weren't right. It was then that we were told there was no heartbeat. Our baby had died. I remember trying not to show how I was really feeling as we were led into the 'quiet' side room. It wasn't ok or the 'done thing' to allow other people to see me break down and weep uncontrollably.

Here, in this bleak side room, we were given our options and expected to decide: wait for things to happen naturally, take medication or have surgery.

I didn't feel able to 'sit and wait'—it felt too raw and hard. Just that weekend, my morning sickness symptoms had ramped up. I couldn't sit and feel pregnant when I knew I was waiting for something very different. So, we chose surgery and were sent home to wait for an appointment.

Two days later, I went into day surgery, greeted by a lovely nurse with, 'Good morning, so what are we in for today?'—clearly expecting an in-grown toenail or something, not, 'We've lost our baby.' Cue hours of waiting and being made to feel like an inconvenience (they needed to deep clean a theatre ready for me as I have a latex allergy). One department blamed me for having an allergy and moaned that they hadn't been told—hardly a caregiving environment that day! Finally, I was called to surgery. I was kept lying and waiting in a holding area for a good hour or more. Here I broke. I was shattered into a million pieces but felt I should stay contained and quiet. I didn't let it show.

A surgery nurse checked my chart and called to her colleague, 'We need surgical waste disposal for this one.' I wanted to scream, 'That's my baby!' but the thin thread by which I was holding it all together would have snapped. I remember a male nurse wheeling me into theatre and chatting about Bake Off. How I had a normal conversation about cake I do not know! But I felt that, if I allowed myself to really connect with what was happening, I would have been hysterical and inconsolable. This was my baby. This was *our* baby. Our creation together. Someone who, from those early thoughts, brought joy and terror in equal measure. I had already fallen totally and completely in love with the future vision of us as a family. But now, this vision was waste.

I came round to an empty recovery room. Barely awake for five minutes, I was asked, 'Do you know where you are going from here? Which department is taking you?' *How should I know?! I was the patient!* I was quickly wheeled back to day surgery and met with, 'Well, she can't stay here; we're all going home.' In my groggy, painful state, I was aware of being unwanted—a burden to everyone in the hospital. My pain an inconvenience. So, a dark and empty side ward was found for me to wait until I felt ready to go home. ('Just get dressed and head off when you are ready.') I was told I couldn't even put the lights on because I wasn't supposed to be there. I sat, waiting, until I felt able to stand and get dressed. Wanting to cry and ask for help. Wanting to be offered support and assistance. But there was none to be found.

Looking back at this experience (which left me a shell of who I once was), I wish that I had allowed myself to feel, both at the time and afterwards, instead of pushing it all down, becoming bitter and angry. I wish I gave myself time to grieve, to take the time and space I needed to feel what I had lost. I would have been harder to be around for my family, but instead I protected them—and myself by not truly feeling all of what was happening.

I wish that I'd used my voice. That I had spoken up and spoken my truth. I have always advocated for others, but when I really needed to do so, I couldn't do it for myself. I know that, in the moment, the voice would have been angry, sad and probably would not have made much sense. But maybe someone would have listened and seen that I was not OK. I was struggling. Underneath it all I was drowning.

What I didn't realise is how much this day would impact my life going forwards, how it would guide my choices.

I struggled for a long time with being visible and using my voice. I am a holistic photographer and struggled to share my work, my creations. My 'creation'—my baby—was waste, therefore everything else I created was too! I created a vision of family and of love, and this was waste. I didn't realise that I had held on to this pain in my body. The isolation and grief made me shy away from connecting with my feminine energy and was the cause of the sudden inability to share photos I had taken. How could I share my work when anything I created was waste? How could I share my vision when this was only good for disposal? Because of this, I put my career as a photographer on hold for years. I hid a piece of myself and didn't feel like I could explore this as an option anymore. I put myself back into a box and, in some ways, closed the lid.

After more miscarriages and more grief, I reached a point where I had to rattle the lid of this box. I was screaming to be heard. I stood up for myself, and for my body, and said *enough is enough*! During a long car journey, my husband and I had the difficult conversation about stopping trying for a baby. We were both honest with each other and started to speak our truth again. This wasn't the way for us.

We announced to our family that we were going to an open morning with an adoption agency to learn more about our options. We wouldn't tick the box to be parents the way we were expected to, and I remember this being a difficult conversation.

We knew we wanted to be parents. I knew I wanted the chance to be a mummy, but not at the expense of my mental health and the punishment I was subjecting myself to. I was able to start using my voice again, to admit that I actually dreaded being pregnant; that it didn't feel good or right anymore—there was no joy.

What I didn't realise was that making this decision—connecting into what felt right—would be the start of me becoming who I was always meant to be. I had been utterly broken, but now it was time to rebuild; to put myself back together, to be more beautiful and powerful than before. I am a walking disco ball. A shattered mirror put back together to be brighter and more sparkly than ever. The art of Kintsugi, a form of Japanese pottery, resonates with me. By being repaired, cared for and making considered healing choices, the new 'pot' is so much stronger, more creative, more … well, more than before.

It was an intuitive hit that led to a random Google of adoption agencies in our area. I don't know what called me to make that search, but I know now it was my intuition and soul guiding me. And in that moment, I listened. I am so glad I did.

We took the leap into the adoption process. I have since been asked what it was like, and I tend to answer, 'One of the most intrusive and emotional things we have ever done.' And this comes from someone who can count surgical procedures in double figures! It was hard and very introspective; we had to delve deep into our own histories to prove that we could provide the best future for another human being. But I found the process to be healing as well. It made me revisit experiences and connect with how I felt at the time and how they had shaped me. The adoption process allowed me to talk openly and freely with my husband and my family about things I had never discussed before. It gave me permission—permission to be *me*.

Through the process, I rediscovered my inner cheerleader as well as my ability to dream. I knew more than ever that there was a child waiting for us and that we would be incredible parents given the chance. This cheerleader helped me to complete a 100km ultra challenge with my sister the weekend before our adoption panel. She helped me to see myself as a strong woman who didn't belong in a box anymore (although ironically, we had to tick many boxes to become parents).

Once we were approved, everything happened so quickly. Within four months, we brought our eldest home and knew that her baby sister would be joining us within weeks. It was an incredible rollercoaster of emotions. To walk into a room to see a little blonde-haired girl playing, turning to look at us shyly, knowing that we were going to be part of her future—there are no words. After only three days of knowing us, we were 'Mummy and Daddy', being embraced and even trusted enough that she fell asleep on me—totally incredible.

There have been some really difficult times—three-hour outbursts of emotion and difficult questions—but there has been so much joy as well. These two little girls are, without question, our daughters and our family—our vision and dream made real. I know now that I can create something magical and beautiful. I created a family home where we openly say, 'I love you', and where hugs and laughter happen more than cross words and tears. I created a safe and stable place for two little girls to explore and grow and to feel like they belong.

This knowing wasn't instant though. My new self, still fragile, struggled with this new identity of 'mummy'. My cheerleader got drowned out by all the pressure I was putting on myself and I started to lose touch with the intuition and connection that I was discovering.

This time, though, I had little hands holding mine, helping me not to get lost. And I followed the breadcrumbs the universe sent my way to learn something new and to rediscover soul truths I had forgotten.

My spiritual awakening, fully stepping into my true self, began with discovering the Law of Attraction and reading about someone else's path; the synchronicities that showed up for them and the signs that they had followed. This got me thinking and realising how the universe had been showing up for me and supporting me through everything. I discovered journaling and crystals. I reconnected with meditation, and even went on to study to be a meditation teacher and a reiki healer. I rediscovered my soul's path to use creativity and energy alchemy to help women feel more confident. To help women show up in their businesses as their true selves, to live life unapologetically and connected with their inner goddess.

I have found the strength to look back at the past few years and see how I was broken and rebuilt. I could see how this pain had built walls inside me, boxed up my creative and intuitive nature, and blocked the feeling and expression of joy. As I rediscovered my fire, it illuminated these dark shadows —this time I didn't run and hide. I have got comfortable with the uncomfortable and talking to it, coaxing it out of the box and finding a way to set it free.

I hate boxes. I won't be put in one anymore. I have set fire to my box, broken out and feel illuminated. I'm shining bright and, by doing so, shining light on others. I won't put my precious girls into boxes. They don't have to break free. They can be who they are destined to be, and I will cheer them on every step of the way. They can live life doing what they love and being their true authentic selves. I am now showing them how to do this. I am showing them, in my own way, how to be truly you, with ease, flow and love.

About the Author

Katie Felton is a holistic photographer, creative soul and spiritual goddess, as well as a badass wife and mummy, proudly wearing her queenly crown!

Her mission is to help healers heal the world. She wants to help others to have the belief, confidence, self-acceptance (as well as gorgeous brand photography!) to shine their brightest, illuminate their magic, step into their power, and shine their light to the world.

Katie is also a Reiki healer and meditation mentor and is passionate about helping children and young adults develop resilience and strategies, through mindfulness and meditation, to thrive as they grow.

Katie loves to spend her time with her family, a bracing dog walk by the sea and indulging in a cosy pot of tea with a good book.

Connect with Katie:

Website: www.katiefelton.co.uk

Email: hello@katiefelton.co.uk

Me, Myself and The Universe

By Margaret McCallum

'A really strong woman accepts the war she went through and is ennobled by her scars.' ~ Carly Simon

In my late teens/early twenties, you would have considered me happy, ambitious, and confident. This was the illusion I created. I was outwardly confident, but inside I always felt out of my depth. I was smiley and friendly, but deep down, I was lost and unsure; ambitious but self-doubting. I was a small-town council estate girl. I moved to the city, attended university, and rubbed shoulders with people who had gone to private schools, such as Eton and Fettes.

My university experience left me feeling inferior to those around me. I dropped out of my first choice of subjects after encountering the great class divide in the first five minutes of arriving in the Russian language class. I had come from learning less than two full years of the language in a Scottish state school where the Russian teacher retired. He offered me free home tuition (three hours per week) for my Higher because he liked me and knew I would work hard. The truth is, he taught me how to pass the exam. I am ever grateful to him, however, for believing in me. I sat down on my first day at university, and people started chatting. One of my fellow students announced that he had returned from six months of study at Moscow State University the week before.

My French class was no different. I always describe myself speaking French at university as a 'Scottish girl using French words in a Scottish accent '. I interacted with all walks of life and all diversifications. Still, it seemed so surreal to what I had experienced until that point. I did not know how to appreciate or feel part of university life. To fully join in, I would have had to change my thoughts and beliefs, and at that point in my life, I was not capable of doing that—it would have made me a different person. I was worried that people back home would tell me that attending university had changed me.

I was overwhelmed by the whole experience. I created my escape from some of it through necessity. Whilst I was funded by a student loan, I had to top up to survive. So, I applied to work part-time in a cinema. I quickly found that my working life, where the people were working-class, hard-working in the main, and more importantly, more like me, was where I felt most at home.

I was a supervisor within three months of joining, and another three months saw me in the management team. I was the general manager's protégé, and he invested in me by rewarding and sharing expertise and knowledge. I had challenges from people who resented my astoundingly rapid promotion. However, I was thriving in the work experience and social aspect.

Six months later, the general manager asked me to consider a full-time role as a manager, but it would have meant leaving university. I could not do that. I was the first person in my family to go to university, and my dad always told me that once I had my degree, no one could take it from me. So, I declined, agreeing that we could have a conversation again once I had completed my course.

I continued in my part-time role and thrived on the buzz, especially on weekends and holidays. We were a large team of about seventy, working together and playing hard! We would have sell-out crowds come to see blockbuster movies and smash sales targets for numbers of people through the door. We would reach and bust average transaction costs per customer in food and drinks sales. We were a complete dream team. We were motivated by the success we achieved each weekend and holiday period.

A group of ten of us would always head for the city centre's pubs and clubs. We'd stay until closing, and the contracted taxi drivers the cinema employed to get us home on late shifts would pick us up free of charge. We would all go back, drivers included, to someone's house.

On one of these nights, a male colleague assaulted me.

I have never used these words before. I always thought if I said them out loud, I'd be accused of being a drama queen, exaggerating the reality—another indication of my lack of self-worth.

I had gone along to the night out reluctantly. Tension had risen between the man and me before the events of that night, and I had said I was going to pass. A few of the girls had convinced me that there were enough of us going out that I did not need to be in his company. I agreed, so long as they ensured that two or more people were around me for the entire evening. I was aware of him staring at me at various points throughout the night. As the night went on, the stares turned into glares, becoming more prolonged, brutal, and piercing. I ignored him, hoping he would give in and lose interest, knowing he wouldn't.

We had moved a couple of times in the evening, walking from one pub to another. The group ended up in one of the nightclubs. I sat at a row of tables in the club, someone on either side of me, when he leaned over the table and snarled at me, 'What's your problem?' I hadn't spoken or been near him all night.

When I said I had no problem, he leaned his face so close to mine I could feel and smell his bitter beer breath on my face. 'What's … your … fucking … problem?' Now panicked, I tried to stand up, as did the girl next to me, and he swiped the back of my arm and rolled me like a bunny rabbit across the long line of tables. I landed in a heap on the floor but did not stop to take stock of the impact. I bounced up and headed straight for the door. People were yelling, he was yelling, he was yelling my name. I kept running and crying. I was hysterical; I needed to get away from him.

I was protected from further assault by another colleague, to whom I shall forever be grateful. He stepped between this man and me as I tried to call for a trusted taxi driver to come and get me. Three girls took me to my flat. I gathered my belongings for the night and stayed at one of their flats so he could not find me.

I did not press charges as I felt shame—I had once gone on a date with the said man, and when I politely declined invites for further dates and asked if we could be friends, he failed to accept the rejection. He had once arrived on my doorstep with flowers, a box of chocolates, a music tape, a bottle of perfume, and a teddy for my birthday! I tried to reject the offering, and he told me he was simply giving a friend a present and would feel offended if I returned them. Things at work had become increasingly strained, and I was concerned about how infatuated he was. I tried being blunt with him. I tried being kind, but he misinterpreted this as me being interested. I tried being blasé about it, but in truth, I was terrified for my safety—the events of that night confirmed my fears.

When I returned to work the following week, my manager told me they could not do anything about the situation. The night out was not an organised work event. Therefore, they had no jurisdiction over what happened as it was outside company time. I had to continue to work with this man. Far from being supported, I was regularly paired with this man to do tasks by senior managers. These involved me being sent for stock with him in areas of a building that meant that, if he did turn on me, I would have had no way out. They saw it as a game, and I was the entertainment. He used to stand at the doorway to let me know that, if he wanted to, he could stop me from leaving, or choose his next move.

Eventually, one evening after further verbal altercations, he reported me to the management team. He had done it several times since that night to make me look bad (after all, the woman is the one making the scene / creating the drama). The female duty manager told me I needed to sort out the problems between this man and me by sitting and talking with him and to stop letting it affect my work. She offered that she and her fiancé parked issues they had with each other at the front of the building as it had nothing to do with work. All good, but I was not in a romantic relationship with this man. When I refused to sit at a table to chat through the issues, she spat that my stubbornness got me here in the first place. I resigned on the spot—stood up, offered keys, badge, and walkie-talkie, and walked from the building. Those who did have eyes and saw things for what they were pleaded with me to stay and fight. I had no fight left in me.

I returned to the building once more to discuss my 'options' with the general manager. He discussed the same things as before—sit down and talk it through with this man. They claimed to have no evidence to allow them to discipline him, far less sack him.

My bruise, from my shoulder to my elbow … not enough.

The bruises of my brave colleague, protecting me that night in the club while I was used as a human football … not enough.

The tens of witnesses that offered to step forward to confirm my story … not enough.

I was a young female who had been attacked, and the employer's attitude was that it was all hearsay and had not happened on their watch.

So, the only real option was for me to either suck it up or resign. If I quit, I could declare resignation to concentrate on my studies, as I was in my final year at university. My employer promised (doing me a favour so as not to blacken my CV) to back this up when anyone came looking for a reference.

I lost my job, income, and future hopes for the career I had envisioned. Fifteen years on from this incident, I caught up with someone on Facebook who had supported me through that time. He had also experienced being terrorised by the man who assaulted and threatened me. He was gay and another target of this man's testosterone-pumped anger. It turns out that two years after I left, the same thing happened again. The girl complained, but this time they listened to her, and they sacked him.

I have never considered myself a victim but, looking back and being the woman I am now, I realise that this is not ok and how silenced I was through the whole experience. I suppressed my feelings and thoughts throughout the process, and I now know how it affected my self-esteem for a long time.

Even after I resigned, I still had to battle with the male ego. My dad was a protective father, and I loved him for it. The result was that I had not even told my parents about this event. I felt ashamed, as I have mentioned, and I was genuinely concerned about the action my dad might take. I had announced months before that I would be seeking a career in the cinema industry after I had completed my university course. So, I needed to go home and explain why I had walked out of a regular paying job that I loved.

As I had anticipated, my dad exploded, and I could see the rage across his face. No one harmed his daughter and got away with it. No one! So, I spent the whole of the weekend following him around like a shadow. If he announced he was going to the shop, I jumped in the car to go with him—he would not have thought twice about taking things into his own hands to get justice. Interestingly, and tellingly for the time and how we dealt with things, I did not consider going to the police. Even if you were the accuser, going to court brought a sense of shame to the family.

I graduated from university and scraped around to find a decent job. I had no self-worth, and I played safe—the route my career took bore no resemblance to the exciting life I had envisaged. It took me a long time to know my worth, but I know now. I grew as a female, but it took many battles. Externally, people thought I was a strong person who stood up for herself. The truth was that inside I was still a little girl screaming to be heard or seen.

I did not recognise much of the trauma caused by this incident until I invested time and money into myself in 2020. I put myself through a life coaching course, looking at manifestation, the law of attraction, and self-worth. I realised how many times I had played it small in life. I also realised that I had to be a better role model for my daughter and other young females in my life. I tell my story openly, hoping others who have experienced similar situations do not have to wait thirty years to resolve the impact.

I am a self-belief warrior and believe in being you in all your glory. No longer do I seek approval and happiness from external sources. As a result, I have written a book, sold art, and returned to a career that I loved. I am now valued by those around me because I value myself. I have a fantastic network of friends who are positive-minded and supportive of each other. This is the tribe I thrive in.

Now is my time. I am grateful for my life, and I attract happiness to it. I still practice many things my life coach taught me, especially journaling. I've added to them and now provide courses for others based on the things that helped me find joy. I now say the words and believe them—*I am enough, I am* more *than enough!* I want to share with everyone that you can be happy simply by believing you are worthy of it and choosing to 'be more you'.

About the Author

Margaret McCallum is an emerging artist, author, commercial contract manager, and mindset mentor.

Margaret runs workshops and courses using mindfulness and creative journaling, letting people take back the power to recognise and like the reflection in the mirror.

In October 2021, Margaret wrote and illustrated her debut children's picture rhyming book, *My Little Birdie Told Me All About Colours* (TAUK Publishing), which hit Amazon Bestsellers' top ten nursery rhymes. Her art has been exhibited at the M.A.D.S. Art gallery in Milan and Fuerteventura. In her spare time, Margaret loves to walk, kayak, paddleboard, wild water swim and read.

Connect with Margaret:

Website: www.leloftdart.com

Facebook: www.facebook.com/livinglifeinhappiness

Instagram: www.instagram.com/the_be_more_you_creative_guru

Journey of Faith - Finding the Confidence and Resilience to Overcome Boundaries

By Maz Ali-Haynes

'Turn your wounds into wisdom and your stumbling blocks into stepping stones.' ~ Robin Sharma

I was born to second generation Indian parents in the UK, raised by my grandparents until I was five years old. Being the first grandchild, I was treated like a princess. I remember feeling so loved, cared for and nurtured; great things were expected of me. Then, my grandad died.

After Grandad (Nana) passed, life was different. I became the stability for my grandma (Nanny). Wherever she went I was close by. We came as a pair unless I was in school. She taught me the love of sewing and cooking. She taught me to be kind and gentle, just as she was when I was a stubborn child.

From starting school, I realised I was different. Girls wouldn't be friends with me. Aged five, I remember a group of girls going round and saying, "Where are you from?" I just remember my family saying India so I said, "India," and a girl replied, "Oh yeah, we can't be friends!" And so, that was the start of school and the feeling of not fitting in anywhere.

At secondary school, at around fourteen years old, I contemplated ending it all. I didn't want to live anymore. I would go and sit in the attic, which was stuffed with junk, and think, *how can I end it? What are the ways?* Then I would cry—no young teenager should feel like this. What was so bad to cause these feelings?

I had become friends with a girl who began to emotionally abuse me. I was made to feel like rubbish—nothing—for three years. My early teens, that crucial time when kids are growing and developing.

Somehow, she would get everyone on her side, and I would end up alone. She would whisper to other girls, and they would all look and laugh at me. To this day, I never knew what she said but seeing all the girls laughing hurt terribly. When I tried to make new friends, she would somehow sabotage it and I would end up on my own. I couldn't take it anymore.

As she lived nearby, I was made to go with her (and her family) to and from school. I wasn't allowed to take the bus. I cried to my mum, my grandma and to my dad but they wouldn't listen. Now, if any child was so upset, I would know they were telling me that something wasn't right. I would go to Mrs Monaghan's (Mrs M) office to tell her things that had happened, but as it wasn't physical, nothing could be done. I started to realise that when I showed this girl that she bothered me, she would repeat the bullying more—I wasn't going to let her win. There was only one thing for it: to make different friends.

My new friends loved me for me. It was such a lovely experience. And even though I remember the little sniggers from a few girls, my new friends would notice and encourage me to ignore them. I was still stuck with the 'bully' at registration and form times and so decided to change this. I asked Mrs M something that was unheard of: to change forms! Mrs M was a kind and caring lady; she was there for me whenever I needed her. Even though I had a mum at home, she wasn't always available, either busy with my siblings or in her own world.

Within weeks, I changed forms. I couldn't believe it. The form teacher introduced me and asked if I knew anyone. As I looked around, I replied, "Yes, pretty much everyone." It was a funny time because everyone wanted to know what had happened. *Did your parents come in and ask for you to move? Did something else happen?* They couldn't believe that I had been able to talk to the teachers and get this done.

The girl tried to poison my new class and friends against me, but I already had established friends, so she failed. That's when I realised that there are terrible people but if you can stay away from them, there are many kind angels who are there to help you.

This experience taught me resilience and that if I was persistent, I could achieve what I wanted. Even now, I am still surprised that I approached a teacher to request the move. I am forever grateful to you, Mrs M. You saved my life!

Life got easier. I learnt that I had to persist to get what I wanted and needed, and in the end, high school was pretty fabulous.

***

Going to an all-girls school with a sixth form meant my fate was sealed—I had to go there. The school had sold it as a great sixth form; however, within a few months, I knew it wasn't right for me. The teaching and what we were learning was not at an expected standard. I remember looking at books and trying to learn things that weren't taught to us but that we needed to know.

By the end of the first year, one of my friends changed to a prestigious college in Manchester. She got me an interview there and I was offered a place to start in September. I was so grateful that they could see potential as they were very selective with who they accepted.

My mum suspected something was going on and, when I told her I wanted to change colleges, she wouldn't let me. I needed her permission, and she wouldn't give it. She didn't want me to go to a mixed college and so I had to give up the place.

As a seventeen-year-old I had no choice but to listen to my mum, but this was a big learning curve for me. I realised that my mum was not thinking of my best interests but was more worried about what others would think.

I carried on at sixth form, barely passing. My A level grades did not match the expectation based on my GCSE results. You would have thought that something dramatic had happened, but it was merely terrible teaching.

I had decided on a sandwich degree at university, which required extra grades that I didn't have. I had a keen interest in computers and loved using my computer and discovering what I could do with it. I would read computer magazines and learn the tips and tricks from it. There was no YouTube back then, so magazines were the way to learn—I loved it.

I intuitively knew that this was the course for me and that I would gain the desirable experience in my third year. Thankfully, my mum was supportive (although she did ask me if there were any girls-only universities).

I had to phone the university on results day, begging, telling them that my results weren't the best but to please let me in. I was persistent and explained how much I wanted to do the degree. And you know what? They did. I couldn't believe it. I was going to university! The first female in my family to do so. Another example where, with persistence and resilience, I achieved what I wanted.

I didn't realise that computing was a very male-dominated profession, so I turned up at the lecture hall to find around three hundred guys and a handful of girls. This was a challenge and a culture shock for me. All the girls stuck together and looked out for each other—we all became great friends.

The first year went by quickly and in my second year, as my placement got closer, the IT industry came to a standstill. Most companies put a job freeze in place and placements became scarce. I had to be near my family home so applied for commutable jobs but was not getting anywhere. I went to see the lecturer who allocated the vacancies that came in based on the student's interests and location. Every week, I was at her door, asking if anything had come in, but there was a shortage of vacancies and those that came in were either too far away or unsuitable.

The week before the placement deadline where failure would mean going straight into the final year, I was resigned to my fate, but intuition made me turn up at her door as usual, just in case.

The lecturer was really happy and said, "I've just received a new opportunity, give me some time to look through it." After what seemed the longest lecture ever, I went back to her office, and she told me a large bank had sent through some vacancies. I suspected that it would be too far away, but it turned out to be only a few miles from my home.

I went for the interview and was swiftly offered the job. I was nervous and excited all at once as I'd wanted this placement so much. Little did I know that life was about to change.

The following week, I started work. Sat opposite me was a young guy, confident in himself, knowledgeable and helpful. He asked a lot of questions about me, genuinely showing an interest and we began to meet outside of work. He was kind and always respectful. I knew at some point that I would have to decide about us, whether we had a future and what would happen with my family. It meant choosing between my love for my family, or the man that I loved.

It was a tough time. I had to dig deep and decide what future I wanted: one chosen for me by my family (and how it looked to the outside world), or one with the man who was not the right colour or religion. All I knew was that I needed to do something that was for me. I had to decide, *does this work for me, my beliefs, and between me and my God? Could I live with this decision?*

I was not in a healthy situation at home. I was being held back. Decisions were made that were cultural and based on what people would say, not what was right or best for me. We got engaged, and then married! I really did marry my best friend, my love and the most supportive person I know. (Nearly twenty years on, we're still together, happy, and with four beautiful children.)

***

We started a family. We loved being first-time parents and looking after our beautiful daughter. In time, we decided we would like another baby. And so, a new journey began… .

Months passed and I started to think something might be wrong, but as we had a baby already, frustratingly, there was not much the NHS would do to help us. We started to look at fertility treatment privately; the prices were mindboggling. I started to read other ladies' fertility stories on the internet, concentrating on the many successes. It was amazing, finding these women at different stages of their fertility journey and some talked about their experience of going abroad for treatment. I hadn't even considered this or thought that it was a possibility.

I started to do more research. There were many options abroad and I had to go with my feelings and intuition. I began reaching out to clinics with one responding immediately; they were really thoughtful, caring and understanding. They were very positive and looked at all of my tests and the information that I gave them. I felt seen and heard. When I researched and heard about other things that might help, the clinic would agree or tell me other options. Many times, I wanted extra tests or treatments, and they would say, "No, it's really not necessary." I knew that they genuinely cared about their patients' needs and were not simply trying to make money.

Our journey to visit the Czech Republic began with the first of at least ten visits over eighteen months. We had two IVF cycles and I responded well to treatment and the medication. The injections weren't pleasant; however, I visualised my baby and, at this point, was dreaming about twins. With fertility treatment, twins and multiple births are high, so they limit the number of transferred embryos. The clinic was great and allowed me to transfer two embryos. Sadly, the first IVF did not work, and we started another round.

The second IVF cycle didn't take either. By now, I felt drained from all the cycles, medication, vitamins, acupuncture, treatment and everything in between, all while looking after a toddler. We decided to take a break as it was overwhelming emotionally and financially.

One night, a few months later, I realised my period was late. I found an old pregnancy test and had the urge to use it. Two lines appeared straight away—I couldn't believe it! Shocked and surprised, I phoned my husband (who was working away) to tell him. My daughter was asleep in bed, and I didn't want to wait until the morning to do another test, so I woke her up, bundled her into the car and drove to the twenty-four-hour supermarket.

I took the test and there was the treasured word: 'PREGNANT'. Next morning, I called the doctors' to make an appointment. I would have to wait until twelve weeks for a scan. Naturally, I couldn't wait. I looked into private scans and found one that could be done at six weeks. We booked it and it still felt like a long time, but we got there.

At the scan they told us there were 'two in there'. I looked at my husband and said, "Two what?" (This still makes me laugh to this day.) He looked at me and said, "Twins!" I couldn't believe it! The pregnancy was high risk involving fortnightly visits to hospital, but we were blessed with identical twin girls. They truly are my little blessings. We were happy and content with our three girls.

Nevertheless, I still didn't feel entirely complete. I was exhausted from the fertility treatments, and I couldn't face deciding to have another baby after going through everything that we went through.

Around two years later, my period was late again … and I got those precious two lines. However, something didn't feel right. I went to hospital for scans and found out that the baby had stopped growing and miscarried. I opted for a D&C (dilatation and curettage) and that was the end of that. We had very real discussions about another baby, and although I kept saying, "I don't want my fertility journey to end this way," we decided that we would be happy with three children and that our life was full. A fourth child wasn't meant to be.

Surprisingly, I got pregnant again naturally, and in January 2019, we were blessed with a beautiful baby boy—now our family truly *is* complete! Each day is a blessing, each day is a challenge; each day is something new, exciting and filled with love. My cup is full—I am so blessed.

My biggest learning through all of this is: be persistent, be resilient, and carry on, one step at a time. Go for your dreams, no matter what people say. Do what you feel is right for YOU and YOUR future. This is not being selfish; this is putting your oxygen mask on first so that you can help others.

About the Author

Maz Ali-Haynes is a female entrepreneur, home educating mum of four, wife, and a cheerleader of female success for her family and friends. You will find Maz helping and supporting her fellow fempreneurs.

Maz has created a personalised and bespoke sweet gift business called Groovy Treats, making fully personalised sweet items including sweet hampers, sweet cones, party and wedding favours, and business branded treats.

Maz is a qualified NLP and hypnotherapy practitioner and has a keen interest in self-development to help herself and her family. Maz is currently undertaking her coaching accreditation, and is looking forward to sharing this in the future.

Connect with Maz:

Website: www.mindsetmaz.co.uk and www.groovytreats.co.uk
Facebook: Maz Ali-Haynes
Email: Maz@mindsetmaz.co.uk

One Foot in Front of the Other

By Katie Duxbury

'Knowing others is wisdom, knowing yourself is enlightenment.'~ Lao Tzu

It was a sunny day in April 1973. I was a little over six months old. Yesterday, I had played a game. I sat in my play pen holding the bars with both hands, my chubby feet pressed against the bars too. On one side of the room was a glass partition—all the rage in the 70s—the glass a series of large, irregular bubbles. Yesterday, the light from the front window created a crescent on the top of each bubble. Holding the bars I could lean back and watch each crescent of light slide down the far side of the bubble. Then, if I slouched, the light would continue to slide down, eventually pooling in the bottom of each bubble, creating the impression of scales, like on my brother Andrew's dinosaur. The real game was to then quickly

straighten up and catch the light out as it leapt back up to the top of each bubble in the blink of an eye.

Today was different. Today, something was 'off'. The light was perfect, the glass was the same, but my body was heavy and slow to respond. Each time, the light beat me at my game. This wasn't the deal; I should be the winner—I was faster than light yesterday.

As I squinted and tried in my infant logic to fathom the change in dynamic, my eyes felt stuck. Not sleepy stuck, like the times I needed to wake up, but an 'unblinkable' stuck. I felt the need to nod my head to get my eyelids to close.

Unbeknown to me, I was being watched. When I realised Mum was there, I looked to her for help or an answer of some sort. Instead, she looked sad. Somehow, without meaning to, I had upset her. My sluggish body and lazy eyelids had been the reason, I was sure of it—as sure as an infant could be.

A few weeks later, I was diagnosed with Familial Hyperkalemic Periodic Paralysis. This rare condition is often accompanied by myotonia (unwanted muscle contraction) in the eyelids, a dead give-away for my mum who, having seen my staring eyes that same day, realised that, once again, this rare and incurable condition had been passed on. It was the day my mum had been dreading. And the day I came to the simple conclusion that being like this made people sad.

Growing Up With a Broken Body

So, here's the science bit to break down the words:

Familial = passed on through your genes
Hyper = too much
Kalemic = related to potassium
Periodic = not all the time
Paralysis = no muscular movement or electrical response.

The condition is extremely rare and therefore not well researched or understood medically. As far as I am told, there are only two families with the genetic condition in the UK.

So what does this all mean?

Well, as a child growing up it meant being bullied in primary school for running around in the playground one minute, and then not able to walk unaided the next. It meant being called a 'spastic' and having moronic groaning directed at me, just out of earshot of the teachers.

It meant being called a liar for 'making it up' or 'putting it on' as the condition was transient, unpredictable, and otherwise invisible. It meant sitting in the hall crossed legged for assembly and, an hour later, watching everyone else file out whilst I waited for a teacher to help me to my feet and stumble back to the classroom.

It meant teachers rolling their eyes as they failed to understand and (I assume) disbelieved the periodic nature of the episodes.

It meant sitting at the dinner table after an hour playing out, and then having to crawl upstairs on all fours to get to bed.

It meant waking up at night completely paralysed, with the exception of my rib cage and heart muscle, beating ten to the dozen with claustrophobic panic.

As a teenager, it meant arriving at secondary school and being assigned to the low academic groups as the school nurse had confused this neurological condition with a learning disability.

It meant hiding my disability from my friends, for fear of a repeat of the bullying meted out in primary school. I would make excuses to avoid certain activities, *anything* to maintain my secret. My friendships felt fair-weather and superficial.

It meant memorising the terrain of my large secondary school so I could avoid steps and stairs, using the ramps instead. It sometimes meant that I moved around the school at non-peak times to avoid being caught out by curious friends as I struggled with poor accessibility, and then being caught out by teachers for being late.

It meant skipping the audition for the school play as the performances would have involved steps and stairs, even though I had a cracking voice and knew basic tap and ballet.

It meant extreme stress-induced episodes at exam time, finishing a three-hour paper to realise that I had no electrical response below the waist.

The Breakdown

Somehow, through all of these obstacles and against the odds, I managed to pass my A levels and qualify for university. I went to university with a clear plan—one that began to form when I saw my mum's friend in hospital three years before. She'd had a nervous breakdown (although I wasn't told that at the time). The visitors' lounge was desolate and dreary, with a sense of foreboding hanging in the air. At the time, I got the sense that no one really knew how to help her. She was waiting for things to get better, to feel more manageable and, in the meantime, was heavily medicated. My plan gained further clarity when I saw many other instances of mental distress in school friends over the years: anorexia, abuse survivors, loss and bereavement, unwanted teenage pregnancy, domestic violence, still births, and postpartum depression. Many of these situations were dismissed as unavoidable 'women's problems'. Any medical support available was often crude and ineffective.

I started my psychology degree with the ultimate aim of opening a clinic specialising in a holistic approach to women's mental health. At that time (late eighties), Western culture deferred to medics and lacked the research data we now have about the importance of mental and spiritual health. This simple concept was a new idea and yet as old as the hills in Eastern cultures. I innately knew that a combination of relevant therapy, physical care and medical intervention (only if it was necessary) was the key to improved clinical outcomes. I had a fire in my belly with a burning desire to help. I didn't want women to be permanently scarred by their experiences, patched up and pitied for the rest of their lives. I wanted them to thrive again, to find more strength because of their trauma, not despite it.

The trouble was, I quickly realised the course I was doing wouldn't give me the life skills or formal qualifications I needed to succeed and bring my dream to reality. So, my game shifted and became one of surviving three years of curriculum and not disappointing my parents. I could then figure out Plan B with a degree under my belt.

Then, life decided to deal her cards! A new relationship, major operation, miscarriage, wedding and failed grant application all culminated in me losing my place at university with only eight months to go. On the one hand, I was relieved because I knew the qualification would really just be a piece of paper. On the other hand, however, I felt embarrassed at having failed and had even less idea on how to achieve my goals.

By my twenty-first birthday, I was a married woman with no profession, no degree and very few prospects. Relations with my parents were strained and the only thing I was passionate about was hating my job. Through all this, there were so many layers of subterfuge and strategies to deflect, hide and obscure my disability that I completely lost sight of who I was. I didn't even have the courage to try to be someone else. Who could I role-model to? No one else had my unique set of circumstances. I gave up on my dream of helping other women and buried it deep. After all, who was I to suggest that I could change someone else's life when I couldn't even get a grip on mine?

Breaking the Cycle

When I thought all hope was lost, life still had cards to deal, this time creating more alignment than I would realise. I was lucky to have picked a life partner who wanted more from life and, like me, had a massive desire to help others. Somewhere along the line we ended up with a copy of *Dianetics, the Modern Science of Mental Health (c)*. If you are not familiar with *Dianetics,* it was written in 1950 by L. Ron Hubbard, the *Pulp Fiction* author and philosopher. It documents his research into the mind, which he originally began to assist US war veterans. It proposes that the mind is made up of two parts: the reactive mind (primitive in nature and formatted as a stimulus/response mechanism) and the analytical mind (an accurate computer that effectively solves the everyday problems of living). (I use the word *proposes* because, at the time of reading, this was just another book that had lots of theories and ideas that sounded great on paper).

It wasn't until my husband had met a Dianetics counsellor and had his first therapy session that this little book, written decades earlier, began to stand out from the rest. He read the book cover to cover, daring to hope that the scientific nature of the technique and the simplicity for the concepts might actually work. Well, the session was textbook and, within a couple of hours, my husband had addressed an area of his life that had bothered him for years.

The Breakthrough

In the handful of years that followed, we learned more about the Dianetics community in Manchester and began to read more about L. Ron Hubbard's Scientology research. (Dianetics counselling is directed to the reactive mind and lessening its impact on the ability of the analytic mind. Scientology therapy is directed to you as a spiritual entity, above and beyond the mind and the body).

Around this time, the biggest lightbulb moment for me was exploring the anatomy of the Parts of Man. Ron taught me, contrary to common parlance, that you don't *have* a soul, you *are* a soul. Whether you use the word soul, spirit, life-force, entity, it doesn't matter. We are all spiritual beings who love and sometimes hate, have ideas, create art, have unique viewpoints and opinions, imagine tall tales, compose music, and have empathy for others. Alongside this we have a mind, used to compute and solve problems, and a body through which we communicate.

Simple as this concept was, I felt like my whole world had come into focus. I wasn't defined by my body; it was a piece of machinery which sometimes let me down. I suppose it's similar to driving a car—it doesn't matter if I was to drive a top specification Bentley or a beat-up wreck, it's still me doing the driving, still me in charge of the direction of travel. All the worry, angst, and need to hide the condition for fear of judgement just drifted away. It didn't matter anymore.

Alongside reading as much as I could, I put in the time to work with a Scientology counsellor. Together, we have ad hang-up on communication and public speaking. We have looked at areas of immense frustrations in my life, circled around the problems and unpicked them to a solid resolution. We have analysed times of extreme guilt and regret, when I have compromised my integrity and, as a result, minimised my power. We have pored over seemingly inexplicable incidents when I have unconsciously allowed my reactive mind to take over, setting up future tripwires that would eventually trigger me without warning. As soon as I can see the trip wire for what it is, it ceases to exist or have any power over my mental health. Some of these sessions have addressed my infancy, including reviewing that time when I was six months old, sitting in my play pen, inadvertently feeling culpable for my mum's feelings. Some have been earlier than that, but that's probably another chapter for another book. The renewed clarity that this style of review gave and continues to give me is mind blowing. Like the realisation that making my mum sad with my slow body led to the conclusion that my condition makes people sad—hiding it was the best way.

And now, as I approach half a century with this body, using Scientology tools every day in every aspect of my life, I can reflect on my struggle with impunity, and truly appreciate what I have gained. Growing up, I knew that I was pretty clever; excelling at academic subjects meant I could be acknowledged for my intelligence instead of labelled as disabled. I now have two vocational degrees and an award-winning career in a field I love. I have a genius level IQ. I'm a strategist, a problem solver.

I learnt tenacity at an early age because I was taught that giving up wasn't an option. I was never allowed to use the condition as an excuse and never expected special treatment because of it. After all was said and done, both my mum and maternal grandmother had the condition and so I was following in the footsteps of two indomitable women. The combination of the fortitude and moral character they instilled in me, and the clarity of thinking that Scientology has unlocked, means that I'm becoming a pretty indomitable woman myself.

I have successfully birthed two amazing humans and held together a thirty-year marriage.

I am proud to be a scientologist, despite weird opinions and ridiculous media propaganda.

I am a fully paid up member of hands down the best Hyperkalemic Periodic Paralysis support group: the inspiring, caring, fiercely intelligent McGregor family, who are all doing amazing things with their lives.

I haven't given up on my original goal of helping women through a holistic approach, which will undoubtedly involve life-changing Scientology tools as part of the solution. I am currently training to be able to administer the counselling to others, so I am a step closer to helping with the deep work too. I may have taken the long way round, but each step, both physically and spiritually, is one step closer. So, I will keep putting one foot in front of the other.

Watch this space.

About the Author

Katie Duxbury has forged an award-winning career in human resources specialising in reward and payroll, holding various corporate roles as well as a period of freelance consulting.

Proudly hailing from Bolton, she currently lives in Cheshire with husband Gary. She has two adult children, both of whom are her favourite (just for the record). As an unapologetic Daddy's girl, the sudden loss of her beloved father in 2021 led her to re-evaluate her priorities and make room for heart-led projects. This book is one of them!

Katie's biggest blind spot is forgetting to take time for herself, something she plans to rectify this year by finishing the fiction book she started writing in 2012. She might even publish it.

Connect with Katie:

LinkedIn: @Katie-duxbury-HR
Facebook: @katie.duxbury.96
Instagram: @duxbury.katie
MeetUp: @BeCause Cheshire

Finding My Own Path

By Maddy Templeman

'You alone are enough. You have nothing to prove to anybody.'
~ Maya Angelou

I was top of the class for every subject, destined for a scholarship to Oxford or Cambridge University, until I started missing school.

I was twelve years old, in my second year of high school, and catching every illness going around. A throat infection would spread to my ear, then to my chest, back to my throat, and so on. I kept getting new sicknesses; my poor body struggled to fight off each one. I soon became rundown and permanently exhausted. I would go into school whenever I felt well enough and catch up as much as I could when I wasn't there. However, it wasn't long before I was absent more than I was present.

At parents' evening the same year, my teachers had said that I would be able to apply for a scholarship to Oxford or Cambridge if I could just attend more lessons. My whole family were delighted and excited at the prospect of a graduate from a top university in their fold. This pressure to succeed and attend school despite being ill only added to my own internal expectation to be the best. Now, you may be thinking that I was a swot and a perfectionist and deserved to have a taste of the real world, and you may be correct! I had been brought up to strive to be a high achiever and not to take second place; this was just part of being me.

As if all of this was not enough, I was also becoming a target for school bullies who decided that being off school and still doing well in tests and lessons was the perfect excuse to pick on me.

After a couple of years, it became apparent that I was not going to get better. My GP had pretty much given up trying to find out what was wrong and even a specialist didn't know why I was ill other than 'school phobia'. I tried to explain that I was not scared of going to school, I was just too poorly to attend, but the specialist didn't listen. Around this time, I read a book about ME (Myalgic Encephalitis), and my symptoms matched it exactly. My GP didn't believe in the illness (very common at that time) but said that it could be what I had. It felt so much better to be able to give it a name, to accept that I would not be going to Oxford or Cambridge and possibly would not be able to attend university at all.

I left school at sixteen years old with only five GCSEs due to the work I had missed. I knew I would have to re-sit, if only to satisfy my own expectations, so I enrolled at a local college. I was still really poorly so it was a struggle, but I managed to pass a few more GCSEs. A year later, I decided to try and obtain some A-levels to get me back on track for a degree. My health worsened, and I became very frustrated as I had already lost so much of my education. It all felt very unfair; I was depressed and upset about being ill all of the time. I missed a lot of the lessons, and after a bout of shingles, I came out with one grade B A-level in English literature. Books have always been an obsession of mine, so it was especially gratifying that I passed that one.

Once I didn't have to go to school the pressure from my family reduced but I was still desperate to try to get back on my career path. I had given up on being a forensic scientist or vet and decided I would do an English degree through the Open University and see where that took me. As I only had one A-level, I had to do an arts foundation year which included literature, music, philosophy, art history and history. I loved it. The tutors gave me extra time when I needed it, I no longer had the stress of trying to attend classes, and I managed to complete most of the assignments. I felt like I was back in control again. My second-year literature-based course was the same—my love of books meant that the reading quota was not an issue and I completed another year using my allowance for late essays to work around being ill.

Meanwhile, my health was continuing to deteriorate. Eventually, I was house bound. The exhaustion was overwhelming, and it was an effort to get out of bed never mind go downstairs. I was falling behind with my studies, and I realised that this was adding to the tension that I was feeling. I eventually made the difficult decision to stop studying. My tutor was devastated as I had been working through a music module and doing really well. I knew I had to think of my health first and I kept hoping that I would start getting better and be able to pick up where I had left off. It was the right thing to do but it made me feel even more of a failure.

After a few dark years of living with a debilitating illness, I gradually started to improve. I found that I could do more, think clearly again, and I was able to leave the house. I decided to take some basic computer courses so that I would have some skills in place in order to apply for a job.

Building Back

When I was twenty-seven years old, I was well enough to start looking for a part-time job. I applied for some secretarial positions and also as an assistant/trainee librarian (I told you I love books). I had to be honest in my CV and say that I had not worked before; surprisingly, I was still offered three interviews. My self-confidence had been knocked massively by being ill and I genuinely didn't think anyone would want me. I remember going into the interviews feeling terrified and completely out of my depth.

My second interview was for a building services consultant (they design the mechanical and electrical elements of a building). I had written under my hobbies that I sang in a blues band and the person interviewing me started off by asking about that. Half an hour later, we were still talking about music. I was relaxed, and it enabled me to stay calm for the whole of the interview. He offered me the job there and then, checked I was well enough to work three days a week, and asked me to start on the following Monday. I happy cried and could not believe that I had been chosen.

I obviously said yes and entered the world of work, scared but excited at the same time. Starting work was a shock; I was not used to waking up early, being around that many people or taking public transport. My mental health was still very low, and I was afraid of wasting the opportunity or letting my boss down. The first six months were a bit hit and miss but I finally started to find my feet. I carried out general secretarial work such as answering the telephone, booking appointments, typing up letters and reports and organising the post run. Then, one day, my boss came in to see me and said, 'You are good with words, from now on you can write the tenders.'

I had never heard of a tender, so I had to ask him what on earth he was talking about. Basically, writing a tender is like applying for a job. A council or public body advertise for something they need to purchase and write a list of questions for applicants to respond to. The applicants answer everything and submit their application then the buyer marks the tenders and chooses the best company for the job. I knew that I could write as I have always written short stories, song lyrics and kept a diary, but this was completely different.

After reading all of the previous tenders, I had a go at writing one myself. The first couple needed a lot of input from my boss, but I soon learnt how to write in that style, and we started winning the work. It was such a boost to my confidence; I felt like I had finally found something I was good at. A few months later, my boss gave me the task of implementing a quality management system and then an environmental system and my self-assurance grew further.

Over several years, my success rate got better, we had a lot of work coming up which we had won through tenders and life was good. Then there was a change in government and the funding for all of the projects was cut overnight. My boss had the awful decision to make some members of staff redundant in order for the company to survive. I was made redundant after nine years of employment and I felt like I was back to square one.

Knocked Down Again

I re-wrote my CV and started to look for a job. To my surprise, I was head-hunted for another secretarial role which involved writing tenders. This was an incredible opportunity and meant that I didn't have to carry on looking for another position. It seemed such perfect timing as I was due to get married three months later so the pressure had been on. However, after a few weeks, it became clear that it was not the right place for me. I was unhappy, felt overworked, unfulfilled and underappreciated. I tried to talk to my employers, but they didn't seem interested. After a chat with one of my co-workers who was also very unhappy, we decided to have a go at running our own tender writing business. We knew other companies offered this as a service; we could write tenders and we were good at it. I also had the money I had received from my redundancy so I figured that would give me a financial buffer if it took a while to get established.

We both left the company, contacted people we knew from previous employment, went to networking events and started to build up some clients. It all started out well, but it soon became apparent that my co-worker and I had very different ideas about how to work with clients. He liked working with big corporates and dressing in power suits whilst talking business speak. I liked working with smaller companies, being myself and still having a laugh whilst getting the job done to the highest standard.

We parted company after a year, very amicably, giving our clients the choice of who they would like to continue working with. It was another big knock to my confidence as I had tried to be more corporate and serious, but I just couldn't keep it up. I had some weeks of self-doubt and lots of trepidation and then, after a discussion with my husband (alias pep talk!), I registered my own business, Templeman Consultancy, in September 2012. I was pleasantly surprised when a lot of the clients chose to stay with me. It turns out that people like working with me *because* I am approachable and good at my job. This has been a huge boost to my self-image and helped me in my journey to believing in myself.

As I had no real idea where to start, I signed up for free business mentoring. My mentor suggested that I offer support to companies with their quality and environmental management systems as this was something I could also deliver. I met a company looking for sub-contractors, signed up and started doing some work for them. I was also getting referrals from existing clients into other businesses and earning a steady income.

I decided to complete several training courses in order to help build my knowledge, so I signed up for a quality management lead auditor course, attended it and passed the four-hour exam (it was quite scary taking an exam again after seventeen years). I have always loved learning, so I continued to further my education with other vocational courses both in person and online. I extended my experience by reading around subject-specific items and watching webinars. You did guess that I was a swot from the start of the story, didn't you?

Another potential revenue stream was delivering training in how to tender. So, I completed my NVQ Level 3 Award in Education and Training so that I could train adults. I wanted to make sure that I could teach others correctly according to their learning style. As a result, I now deliver mixed classroom workshops in tendering and one-to-one mentoring in how to audit management systems.

Here and Now

Fast forward in time and my business was ten years old in September 2022 (there isn't space to tell you all of the gory details of how I got there), I now have a business partner (my husband) and an established client base. I have even managed to consolidate my working week to four days whenever I can.

I once asked my first boss why he gave me a chance when I had no experience and he said that there was just something about me. I will always be grateful to him as the skills and talents he saw and developed in me have enabled me to run a successful business. I am passionate about giving other people the chance I got, seeing the potential and promise in people and helping them to fulfil that. My input helps other small businesses to grow and evolve, to take on more staff and move into new markets. It is an incredible privilege to see the impact that I have on their development.

Although I have struggled with my mental health a lot over the years, having my own business and finding my own educational path has been a huge boost to my confidence. This increased self-empowerment has also helped me to undertake the painful but healing process of writing a memoir about my strange religious upbringing so that it can help others.

I look back on my life and think about how different my journey has been to what I thought it would be. If you asked me if I regret not attending Oxford or Cambridge or completing a degree, the answer would overwhelmingly be no. It may not have been the way I would have chosen at the start, but it has taken me on a unique path, and I like who and where I am now.

As for the future, instead of being scared about what will happen, I am excited to see where life will take me next. I still have my moments of self-doubt, but I am no longer afraid of being seen!

About the Author

Maddy Templeman is a bid writer and business consultant by day, and an author and musician by night (or whenever she can). She is passionate about helping small businesses improve their processes, win contracts and grow. Writing from the perspective of many different companies has brought insight and discipline to her own work.

Maddy is currently editing her first book, a personal account of the alternative Christian lifestyle she was brought up in. She writes pieces for *Broken Spine* poetry and arts magazine, and is an active member of the Pick Up Your Pen writing group. She is also a mentor for The Girls Network and loves to encourage people to reach their full potential. Maddy enjoys reading, camping, walking, travelling, flying birds of prey, and spending time with her cat, Rooster.

Connect with Maddy:

Website: www.templemanconsultancy.co.uk
Twitter: @maddy_templeman
Instagram: @maddytemplemanwriter
Facebook: @MaddyTemplemanWriter

How I Rewrote My Bedtime Story

By Michelle Ewen

'The best bridge between despair and hope is a good night's sleep.' ~ E. Joseph Cossman

'You don't know what 'tired' is until you've had children…' Child-free by choice, I have heard this said on multiple occasions. I simply smile because, for several years, I thought tiredness would kill me. Perhaps I would fall top to bottom down a flight of stairs or step out in front of traffic. Or maybe my nightly 'ungluing' would result in a hospital visit from which I'd never return. Everything seemed possible, except for sleep… .

During my final year at university in 2001, a friend came to stay and commented that I had shouted and thrashed around in the small hours. By that summer, pressing little blue pills past my lips and praying for a 'good night' became a night-time ritual. But it wasn't until two planes crashed into the World Trade Center [sic] and I moved back home for good that my nightly panic attacks really took hold.

Laying in the dark on sweat-soaked covers, fear swept through my body like an electrical fire. An unseen force pulled me upwards by the ribcage—my 'U'-shaped back matching my 'O' of horror. Unable to speak or breathe, I wondered which would explode first: my heart or my lungs? Then, just as I felt myself slipping towards unconsciousness, everything snapped. I was a kicking, screaming, wild person—leaping from my bed and running headfirst into the wall. Sometimes, I would make it all the way down the landing to the top of the stairs, only for my mum to stop me from stepping out into the nothingness at the very last moment.

Lights would ping on in every bedroom and even next door; exhausted figures leaning against doorways, trying to understand what all the commotion was about. I was a mortally wounded ship sinking into the abyss and taking every last passenger down with me. No one slept and it was all my fault.

Once a night would have been bad enough, but it was ten times, twenty times—even fifty. Whenever the elastic tension between wakefulness and sleep snapped, a panic attack kicked in. It happened over and over again, until I was completely jellified—neither a person nor not a person. Just a puddle of water that pooled and separated over and over, until the endless night finally gave way to a new day.

Slipping formal workwear over limbs that were stiff from flailing, I would look into the bathroom mirror and see two black holes where my eyes should have been. There was no glass, in fact. I could push my fingers through surfaces because nothing was real. I was a person commuting via a bus and two trains to do my job at a newspaper, but I was also still face down on the carpet having fallen out of bed. I could feel the velvet-covered seat against the backs of my thighs, but I was also the streak of countryside racing by the window; the woman stood back on the platform; and, at the very same time, suspended in the clouds above, watching myself detachedly.

Time went on and I tried to 'fix' myself. I started having hot baths before bedtime, spraying my pillows with lavender and drinking milky hot chocolate. 'Read until you feel tired', the experts said. 'Do some gentle exercise'. I followed every piece of advice offered and researched more, but I didn't get better. Somehow, my rock bottom had a basement and, below that, another rolling slope straight into Hell.

It was decided that, to minimise the risk of me falling down the stairs, and so that everyone else could at least try and get some rest, I should sleep on our family couch. At least from there, it was only a two-foot drop if I fell onto the carpet. Finding myself face down rigid—my teeth buried in leather and choking on my own screams—wasn't quite the step forward it seemed. With no other options open to her, my poor mum—who was at her wit's end—called out the duty doctor in the middle of the night. He prescribed Valium, which had as much of an effect as a sticking plaster on a severed artery.

During this time, I was in a relationship. On the weekends, I would stay over with my then-boyfriend. He couldn't function on interrupted sleep, so I would lay awake on his parents' conservatory sofa, fighting wave after wave of panic attacks alone in the dark. I was in a state of crisis—trying to hold down a full-time job as a features & magazine editor, heading towards an engagement I wasn't sure I wanted, and all on no sleep. So, when I was offered cognitive behavioural therapy (CBT) on the NHS, I said: 'Yes.'

Of all the days of the week my appointment could have been on, Tuesdays was the worst possible option. That was the day we 'put the paper to bed' (as they say in newsrooms)—preparing it for publication the next day. Still, to his eternal credit and my unending gratitude, my manager released me to go to therapy.

I did not know what to expect and CBT was anxiety-inducing in and of itself at first, but I was willing to try anything at this stage. And so, I found myself talking about all manner of things I had locked inside my internal filing cabinet, never to be spoken of again.

I was born with limb giganticism—a condition whereby my right leg had grown disproportionately in size to my left. It was painful and embarrassing, and the source of much childhood bullying alongside everything from my unfashionable clothes and lack of worldliness to my status as one of the cleverest kids in every class. At home, I was a target for pretty much every local kid on my estate and retreated into a world of make-believe, playing 'house' behind a sheet tacked to the front of our porch, as well as writing stories and creating my own magazines. I couldn't sit on a swing or walk to the ice-cream van without being mocked or jeered at, and I felt weak for never fighting back; guilty for not standing up for myself like my parents wanted me to.

High school and college were my happiest times when I finally made friends who I still love and socialise with to this day. But my university days were marred by an ill-advised relationship I had gotten into just weeks before my first term. Aged nineteen, I started dating a man who was several years my senior. He would go on to psychologically abuse me in every way a romantic partner can. I grew to hate my body, which he told me was unlovable, making cruel and callous remarks that I was too conditioned to even question. The day that relationship ended, just after my twenty-first birthday, it rained heavily. I walked in the wetness and felt nothing, my mind having finally come loose. I took every bad thing that had happened and every hurtful word that had been spoken and poured them into leaking vials of poison, stacked next to my broken heart.

And then, I did what many damaged people do who have lost their self-worth. I fell into another bad relationship. This time, with a man who drove on the wrong side of the road to frighten me, and who shouted so much and so often for every little thing that I shrunk like Alice in Wonderland. I moved in with him when he bought a house. I didn't have a reason not to that I could say out loud; then, I accepted an engagement ring from him in a busy restaurant. (Once you have started to build a coffin, it's easier to keep banging in the nails.)

I started sitting under the dining-room table—staring at the long grass in the back yard that he hadn't and wouldn't ever cut. He never physically assaulted me, but inanimate things were often thrown and punched, so I felt safe nearer to the ground. At night, I was happy to have a reason to stay on the couch downstairs, to not have to sleep next to him—even if that meant screaming alone into the cushions, riding endless waves of panic attacks.

My therapist diagnosed me with panic disorder, a condition whereby you have sudden, successive panic attacks over a prolonged period of time. She felt it was linked to post-traumatic stress disorder (PTSD) and gently held my hand (metaphorically speaking) as I unlocked my internal filing cabinet and faced up to what was inside. It turns out that I had overstuffed my drawers to the point where pieces of paper were forcing their way through the cracks. All the Very Bad Things that had happened over the years were leaking out in the form of panic attacks, because that's the only way my body could process them. No amount of lavender pillow spray was going to solve the problem. It was clear I needed to talk about my buried trauma and find a way to live with it.

In the meantime, I was prescribed both betablockers and sleeping tablets to try to get on top of some of the physical symptoms so talking therapies could work their magic. I saw little to no benefit at first and hated having a constant metallic mouth. It didn't help when I was transferred internally to another newspaper and had to declare my medication. My new boss said that he didn't like having people working for him who were 'on things', which fed into a nagging sense of failure at being medicalised. With time, however, the tablets did start to help, but I was now facing a new challenge…

I had fallen in love with a co-worker who shared my desk. Chris was three-and-a-half years my junior with hair as dark as his eyes. He was intense, talented and kind, and someone who always made me feel safe. We had numerous shared work assignments and started to go on lunch breaks together. When he went to the Coachella music festival in California and no one heard from him for more than a week, I realised in my concern that I cared more for him than a work colleague should.

Chris was in a band, partied every weekend and had a close-knit group of friends that orbited around his star. I couldn't gauge how he felt about me beyond workmates and friends, but I came to realise that good men did exist and no matter whether we were destined to be together, I had to bring my engagement to an end. And so, I did, packing all but the essentials and returning home to live with my parents. I was alone, still seriously mentally ill and lovesick for Chris, but I filled my day with trips to the gym, swimming endless lengths in the quiet pool. I started to notice that I was separate from the water; the world wasn't as liquid. I was coming back to my body and sleeping one or two hours a night.

Four weeks after the breakup, Chris kissed me at a work's party. He asked me to be his girlfriend the following week while I helped him study for a media law exam in the park. Within seven months, we moved into a tiny loft apartment that overlooked the local registry office. On Saturday mornings, newlyweds exited in puffs of confetti while we polished our kitchen to a shine.

Chris knew about my sleeping problems, and he made a rule: no matter how badly I panicked, we would always sleep in the same bed. No more couch or floor for me. Every night, he would put an arm around my waist and bend his knees into the crook of mine. As my body started to stiffen into a panic, he would whisper: 'I've got you. You're safe.' Those five words did more wonders than the thousands I had spoken in therapy. With time, I stopped taking my medication and sleep came to me easier.

That being said, to this day, I still get night-time panic attacks. Any time I don't look after myself—I 'burn the candle at both ends'—they come back with a vengeance. They can last for weeks if not months, and I must work hard at getting them under control. That can involve saying 'No' to social invitations; eating healthier; exercising; cutting out alcohol; or simply accepting that 'this too shall pass'.

But I no longer fear sleep or bedtime. In fact, one of my proudest achievements is building my own business talking about both! In 2015, I quit my job as a communications manager at a mental health hospital and started my own PR agency, Write on Time Ltd. Among my first clients were a bed manufacturer and a bed retailer. I helped both companies to win prestigious awards in their respective fields and have written hundreds of thousands of words about beds and sleeping. I have attended the National Bed Show multiple times, run social media accounts and formed blogging partnerships with leading bed manufacturers. I turned the source of my greatest fear into the freedom to work on my own terms as a successful entrepreneur—all while helping other people to sleep better through advice and education.

These days, Chris and I share our bed with a third living thing: our rescue cat Raymond Reddington. When we first adopted him from Cats Protection, we said: 'No cats in the bedroom,' then a terrorist detonated a bomb at Manchester Arena at the end of an Ariana Grande concert in May 2017. Ray snuck into our bedroom while we watched rolling news coverage and I cuddled him for comfort. He has never left.

Having a sleeping cat at my feet is like balm on my soul. His soft, warm body and rhythmic purrs are the second-best thing to Chris' strong arm. We call Ray our 'therapy cat' and for good reason. I know that panicking will disturb him, which gives me extra strength to fight the urge. On long nights when sleep evades me, I stroke his head and press my face into his back, timing my breathing with his to bring my racing pulse in check. It's often enough to turn my entire night round.

Plus, I am 'doing the work' and finding ways to improve my mindset every day. I can open my cabinet drawers now and look at the Very Bad Things with detachment. I can focus on what I learned from them and let go of the bad feelings. I am thankful that, through my own experiences, I can better understand others with mental health challenges. I am grateful to my family and to Chris for loving me through every sleepless night they have endured, as well as to the friendless little girl who taught herself to write stories. She grew up and helped other women tell their stories, so they feel seen too.

About the Author

Michelle Ewen is a former journalist turned PR pro who co-founded Write on Time Ltd in 2017 with her husband Christian. Together, they have helped more than 3,000 business owners to think of something newsworthy to say and take the first steps towards getting their story in newspapers, magazines, on the radio or TV. Michelle has walked an intuitive path through life—leaving well-paid leadership positions twice and giving up her home once on the same day. Alongside Christian, she was called to complete a world-first voluntary project—telling the stories of 365 female entrepreneurs over 365 consecutive days in exactly 365 words. Now a book and an award-winning blog, #SheCan365 embodies Michelle's complete faith in the universe—knowing things always work out when she acts with courage.

Connect with Michelle:

Website: www.writeontime.co.uk

Instagram: www.instagram.com/WriteonTimeUK

About the Host

Katherine Massey is a Visibility Alignment Guide for women, facilitating powerful and heart-led mentoring and opportunities within her Visibility Queen Academy membership. She retired from her twenty-six-year career in 2017 to write her memoirs, *Living With Dolls: A story of love, mental health and freedom* (published in 2018). As a mental health advocate, Katherine helps and inspires women to go from invisible to visible while sharing her own life experiences.

As the host of *Seen (volume one),* Katherine has realised another of her strengths is to encourage women to recognise the power of their stories. Katherine wanted the next fearless fifteen to be *Seen Too* through their words and hopes that the thirty women that have shared their stories will go on to write their own full memoir one day. Katherine knows that being visible and speaking out can be very hard, but it can also help so many. She will continue to create opportunities for women to be *Seen* and heard.

Connect with Katherine:

Instagram: www.instagram.com/visibilityqueenkat

Acknowledgements

To each co-author who has trusted me with their words, to be seen and leave their legacy within these pages.

To Sue, Estelle, and the team at TAUK Publishing for supporting this process from start to finish.

To Michelle Catanach for her calm, professional and experienced execution of this amazing book.

To Michelle and Christian Ewen (Write on Time Ltd), my VQ Academy membership PR associates, who have delivered exceptional training and support and press releases during this process.

To Naomi Victoria for sponsoring the book launch and making it an extra bit more 'fizzy'.

To the authors of *Seen (volume one)* for your support and encouragement for the *Seen Too* authors.

My deepest gratitude to you all.

Seen (volume one) is also available from Amazon in paperback, hardcover or Kindle: https://bit.ly/SeenVol1

Book Launch Sponsor

Naomi is a motivational speaker, author and mental health awareness and suicide prevention advocate.

Naomi Victoria is proudly sponsoring the *Seen Too* book launch.

"My own life has been far from plain sailing. Now I love supporting others to navigate life's curveballs and discover their own inner happy, to love themselves and love their lives. It's time to drink life while it's fizzy."

Naomi Victoria LTD

Connect With Naomi:

Website: www.iamnaomivictoria.com

Instagram: www.instagram.com/iamnaomivictoria

Printed in Great Britain
by Amazon

10590953R00106